HAL•LEONARD® GUITAR PLAY-ALONG

AUDIO ACCESS INCLUDED

VOL. 182

SOUNDGARDEN

To access audio visit:
www.halleonard.com/mylibrary
Enter Code
5186-9746-3496-1939

Cover photo by Michael Lavine

ISBN 978-1-4950-0235-9

HAL•LEONARD® CORPORATION

7777 W. BLUEMOUND RD. P.O. BOX 13819 MILWAUKEE, WI 53213

In Australia Contact:
Hal Leonard Australia Pty. Ltd.
4 Lentara Court
Cheltenham, Victoria, 3192 Australia
Email: ausadmin@halleonard.com.au

Visit Hal Leonard Online at
www.halleonard.com

Hal•Leonard®

GUITAR PLAY-ALONG

VOL. 182

AUDIO ACCESS INCLUDED

SOUNDGARDEN

CONTENTS

GUITAR NOTATION LEGEND

THE MUSICAL STAFF shows pitches and rhythms and is divided by bar lines into measures. Pitches are named after the first seven letters of the alphabet.

TABLATURE graphically represents the guitar fingerboard. Each horizontal line represents a string, and each number represents a fret.

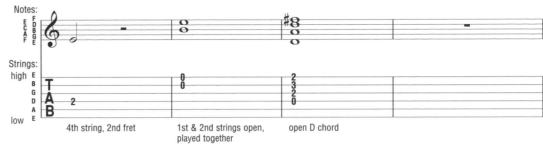

4th string, 2nd fret

1st & 2nd strings open, played together

open D chord

HALF-STEP BEND: Strike the note and bend up 1/2 step.

WHOLE-STEP BEND: Strike the note and bend up one step.

GRACE NOTE BEND: Strike the note and immediately bend up as indicated.

SLIGHT (MICROTONE) BEND: Strike the note and bend up 1/4 step.

BEND AND RELEASE: Strike the note and bend up as indicated, then release back to the original note. Only the first note is struck.

PRE-BEND: Bend the note as indicated, then strike it.

VIBRATO: The string is vibrated by rapidly bending and releasing the note with the fretting hand.

PALM MUTING: The note is partially muted by the pick hand lightly touching the string(s) just before the bridge.

HAMMER-ON: Strike the first (lower) note with one finger, then sound the higher note (on the same string) with another finger by fretting it without picking.

PULL-OFF: Place both fingers on the notes to be sounded. Strike the first note and without picking, pull the finger off to sound the second (lower) note.

LEGATO SLIDE: Strike the first note and then slide the same fret-hand finger up or down to the second note. The second note is not struck.

SHIFT SLIDE: Same as legato slide, except the second note is struck.

TRILL: Very rapidly alternate between the notes indicated by continuously hammering on and pulling off.

TAPPING: Hammer ("tap") the fret indicated with the pick-hand index or middle finger and pull off to the note fretted by the fret hand.

NATURAL HARMONIC: Strike the note while the fret-hand lightly touches the string directly over the fret indicated.

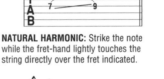

PINCH HARMONIC: The note is fretted normally and a harmonic is produced by adding the edge of the thumb or the tip of the index finger of the pick hand to the normal pick attack.

TREMOLO PICKING: The note is picked as rapidly and continuously as possible.

VIBRATO BAR DIVE AND RETURN: The pitch of the note or chord is dropped a specified number of steps (in rhythm), then returned to the original pitch.

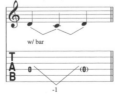

VIBRATO BAR SCOOP: Depress the bar just before striking the note, then quickly release the bar.

VIBRATO BAR DIP: Strike the note and then immediately drop a specified number of steps, then release back to the original pitch.

Additional Musical Definitions

 *(accent)* • Accentuate note (play it louder).

 (staccato) • Play the note short.

D.S. al Coda • Go back to the sign (𝄋), then play until the measure marked "*To Coda*," then skip to the section labelled "*Coda*."

D.C. al Fine • Go back to the beginning of the song and play until the measure marked "*Fine*" (end).

Fill • Label used to identify a brief melodic figure which is to be inserted into the arrangement.

N.C. • Harmony is implied.

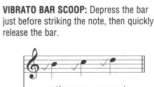 • Repeat measures between signs.

 • When a repeated section has different endings, play the first ending only the first time and the second ending only the second time.

Black Hole Sun

Words and Music by Chris Cornell

Drop D tuning:
(low to high) D-A-D-G-B-E

Intro
Slow Rock ♩ = 52

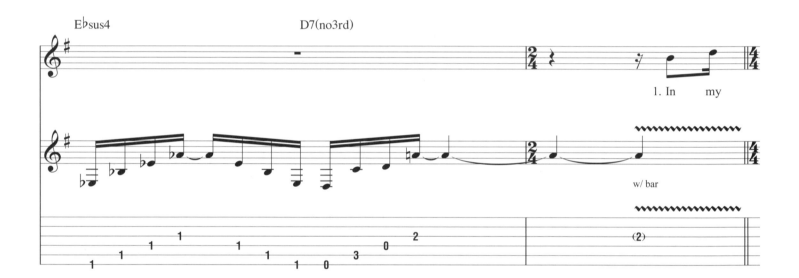

Verse

eyes, in - dis - posed, in dis - guise as no __ one knows, __ hides the face, __
2. *See additional lyrics*

w/ Leslie effect
2nd time, dist. off

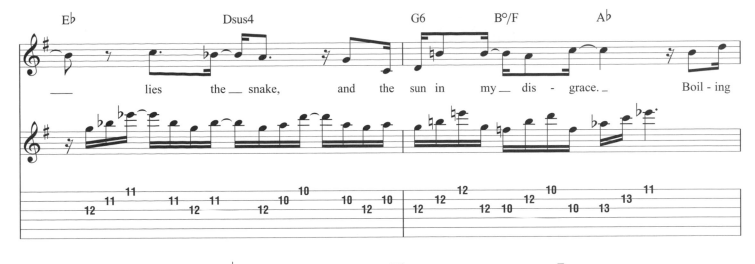

lies the ___ snake, and the sun in my ___ dis - grace. ___ Boil - ing

heat, sum-mer stench. 'Neath the black, the sky ___ looks dead. ___ Call my name ___

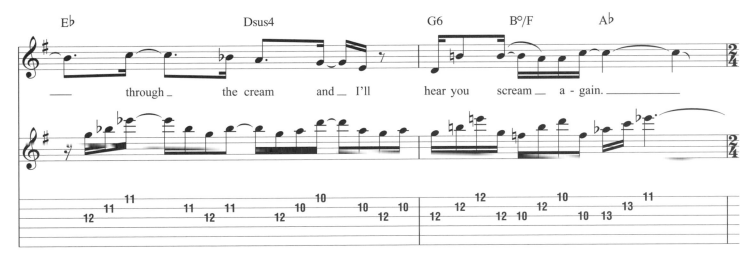

___ through ___ the cream and ___ I'll hear you scream ___ a - gain. _____

𝄋 Chorus

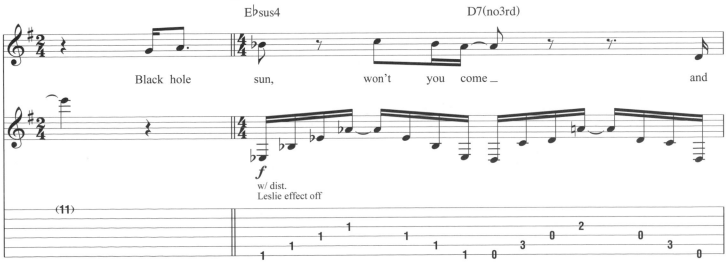

Black hole sun, won't you come ___ and

7

wash a-way ___ the rain? ___ Black hole ___ sun, ___ won't you come? _ Won't _ you come? _

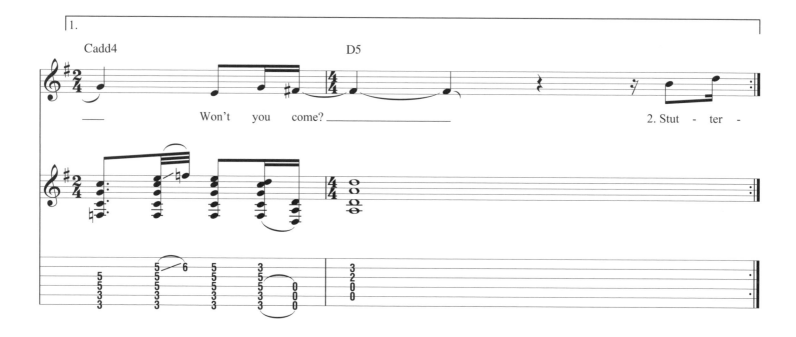

1.

___ Won't you come? _____ 2. Stut - ter -

2.

Black hole sun, won't you come _ and

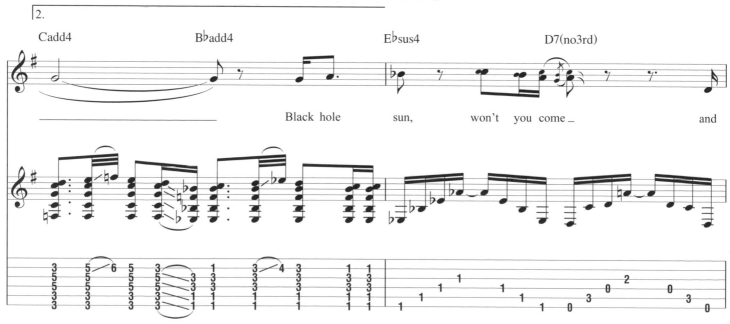

To Coda ⊕

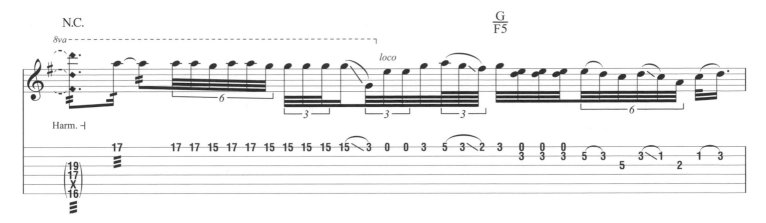

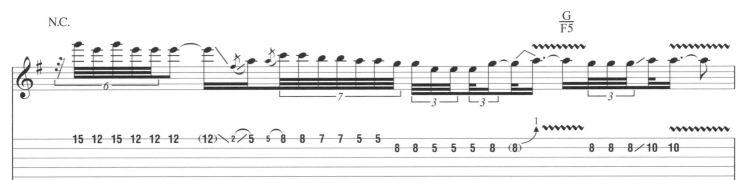

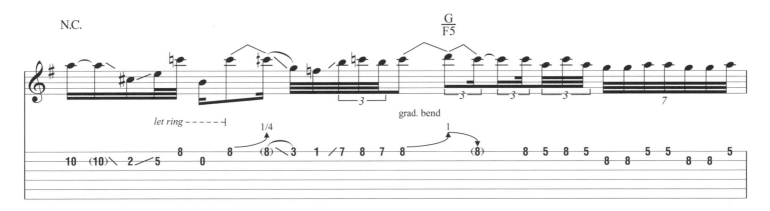

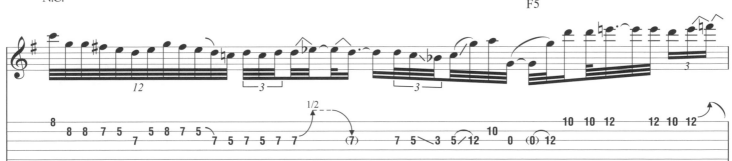

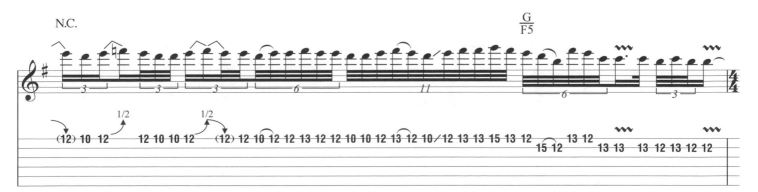

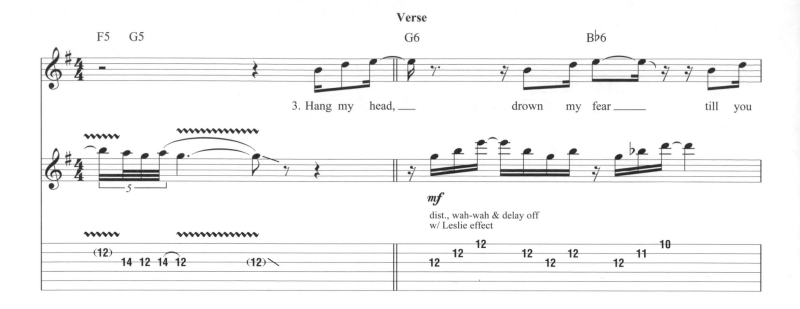

3. Hang my head, ___ drown my fear ___ till you

D.S. al Coda
(take 2nd ending)

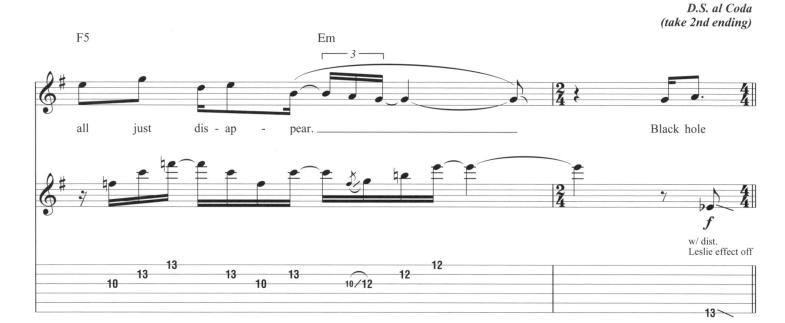

all just dis - ap - pear. ___ Black hole

⊕ **Coda**

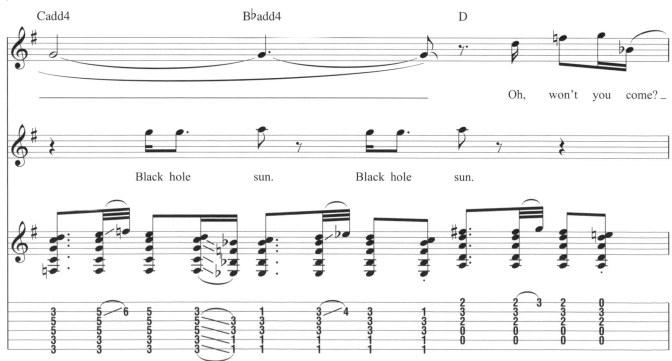

Oh, won't you come? ___

Black hole sun. Black hole sun.

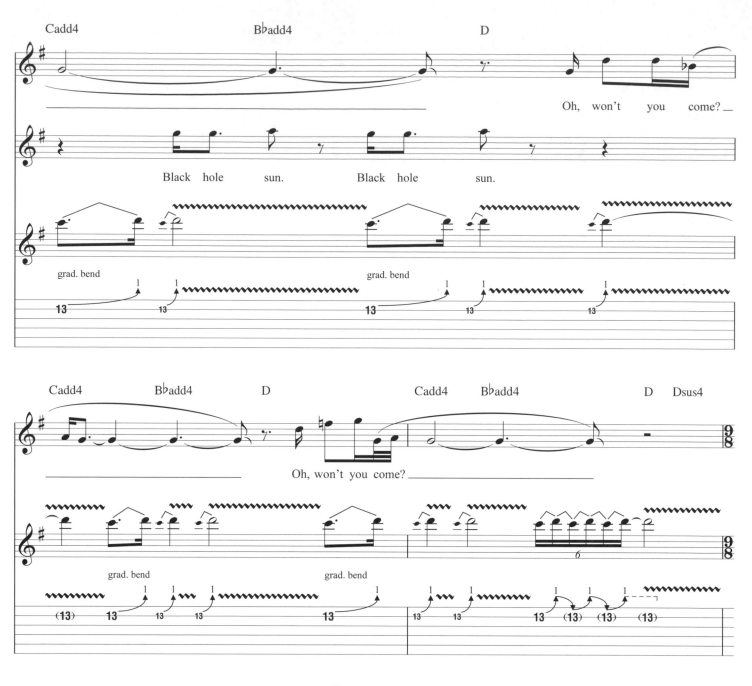

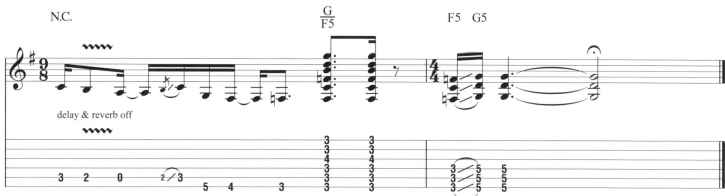

Additional Lyrics

2. Stuttering, cold and damp.
Steal the warm wind, tired friend.
Times are gone for honest men,
And sometimes far too long for snakes.
In my shoes, a walking sleep.
In my youth I pray to keep.
Heaven send hell away.
No one sings like you anymore.

Fell on Black Days

Words and Music by Chris Cornell

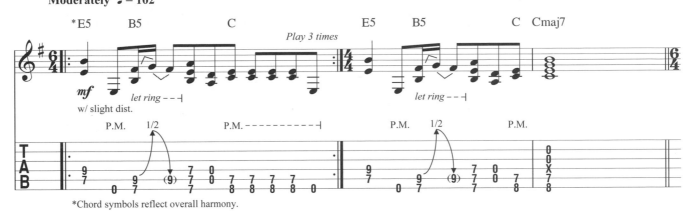

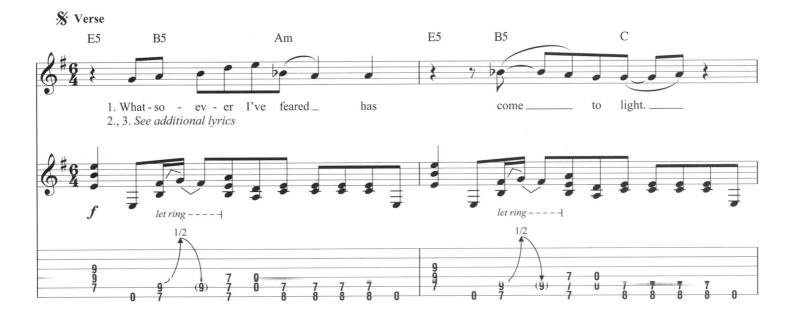

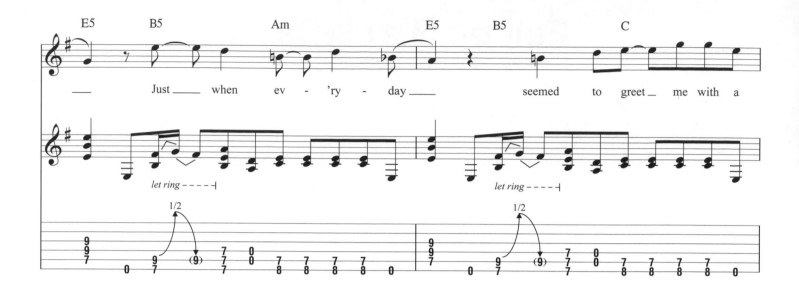

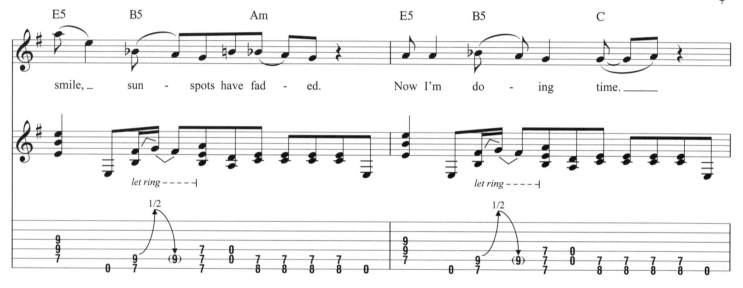

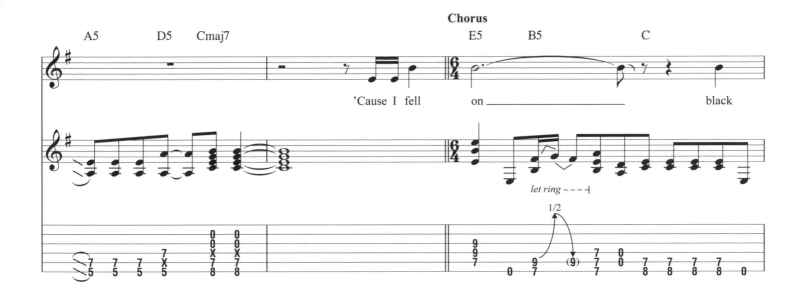

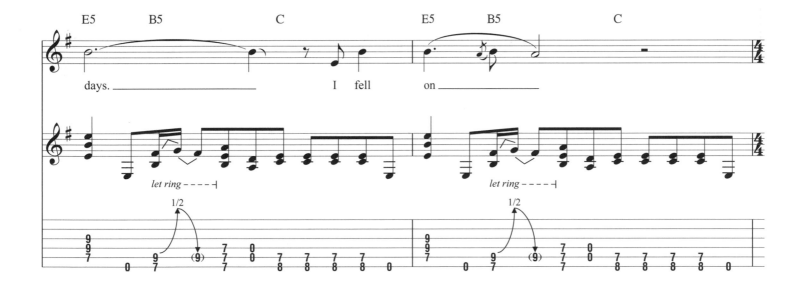

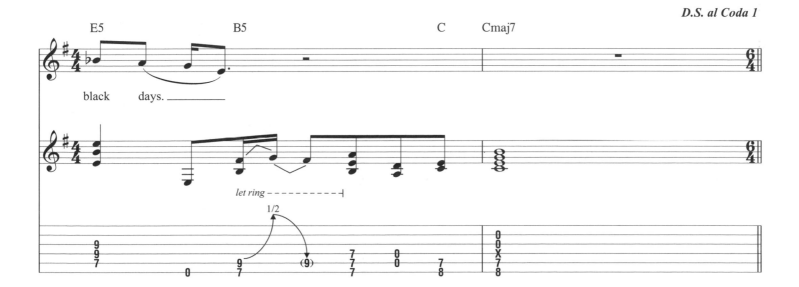

Coda 1

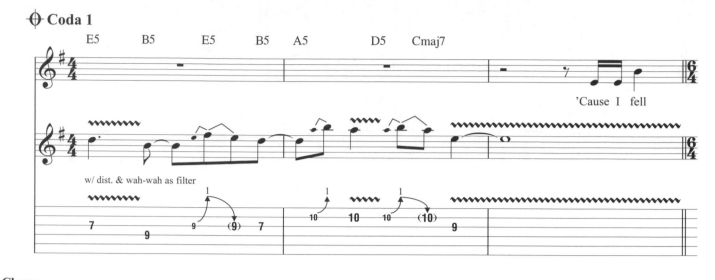

'Cause I fell

Chorus

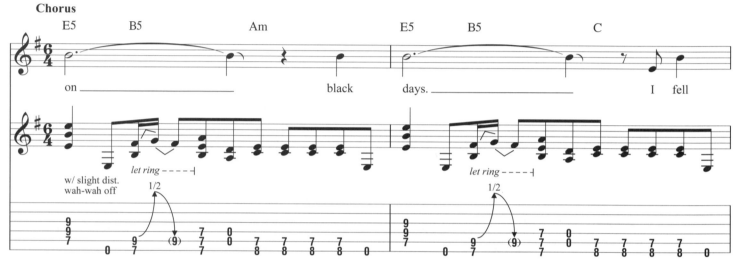

on _____ black days. _____ I fell

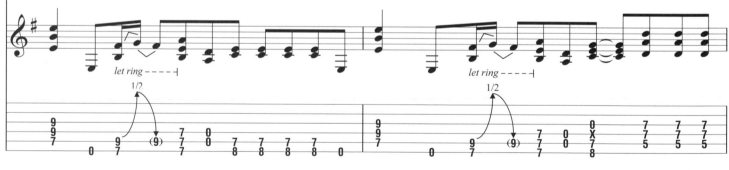

on _____ black days. _____ How would I

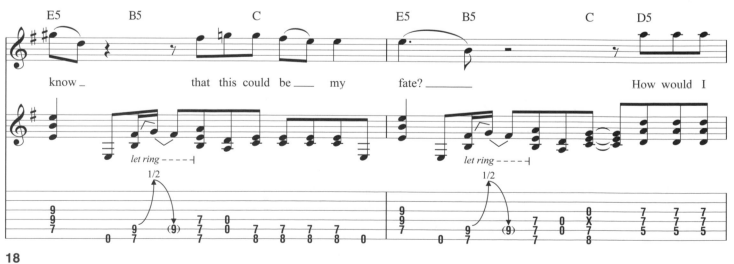

know _____ that this could be _____ my fate? _____ How would I

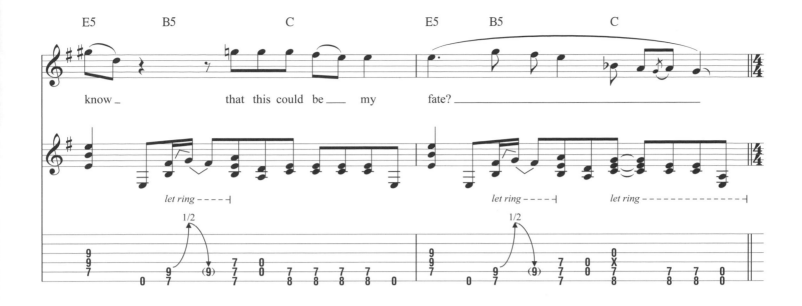

know ___   that this could be ___ my   fate? _____

Interlude

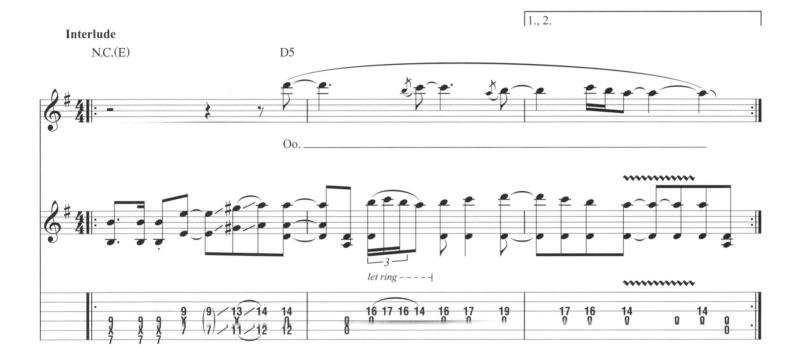

N.C.(E)   D5

Oo. _____

D.S. al Coda 2

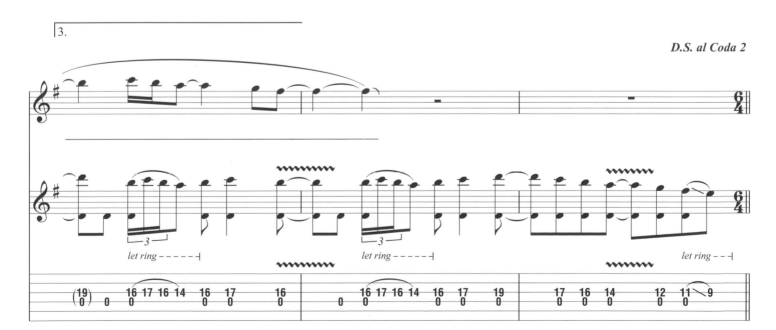

Bridge

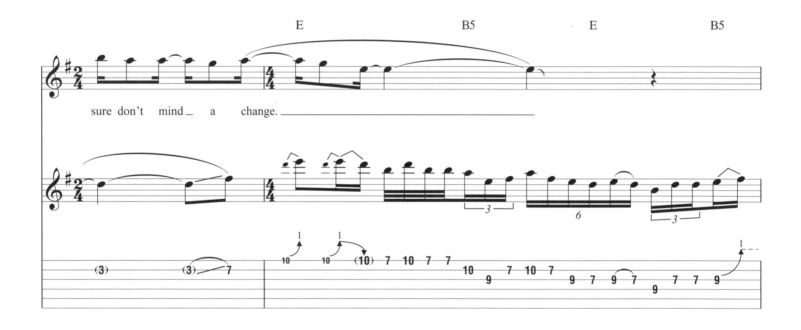

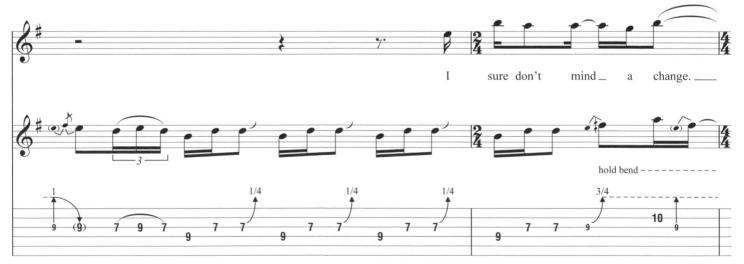

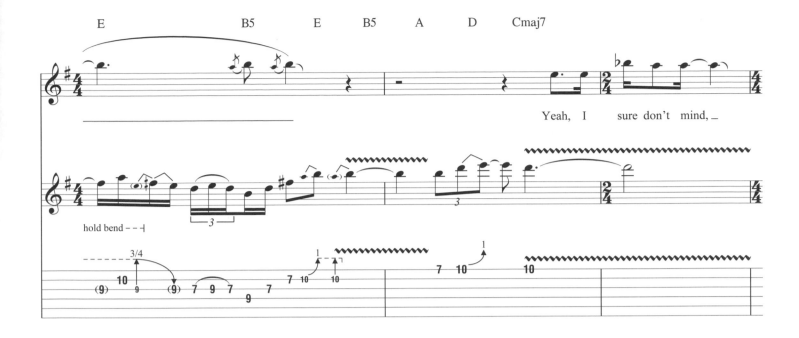

Yeah, I sure don't mind, _

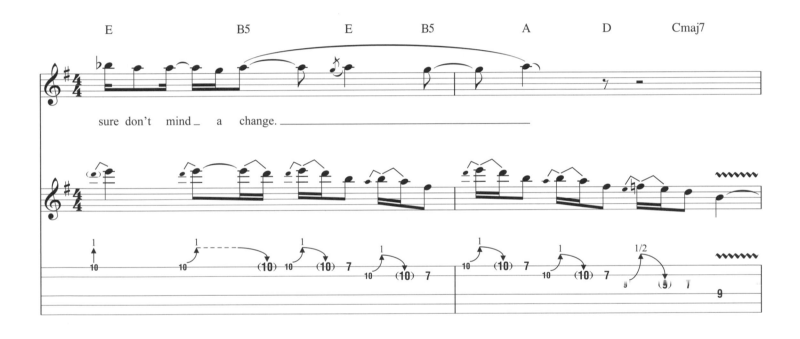

sure don't mind _ a change. _____

Freely   **A tempo**

I sure don't mind a change. _____

'Cause I fell

Burden in My Hand

Words and Music by Chris Cornell

Tuning:
(low to high) C-G-C-G-G-E

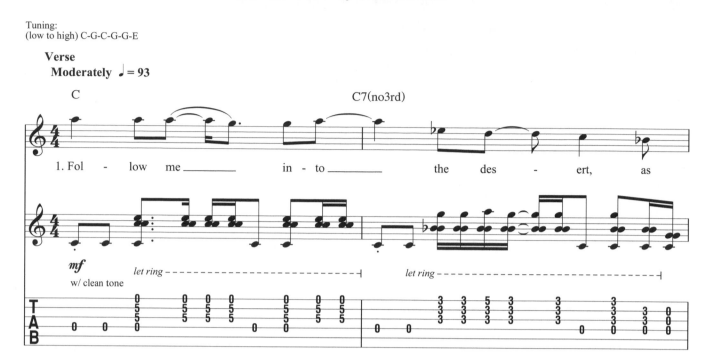

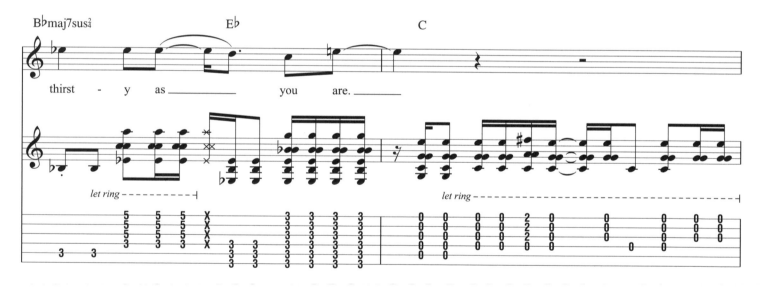

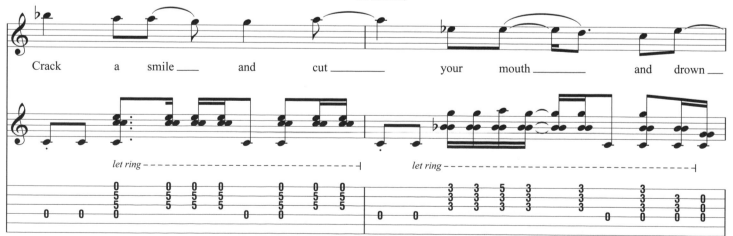

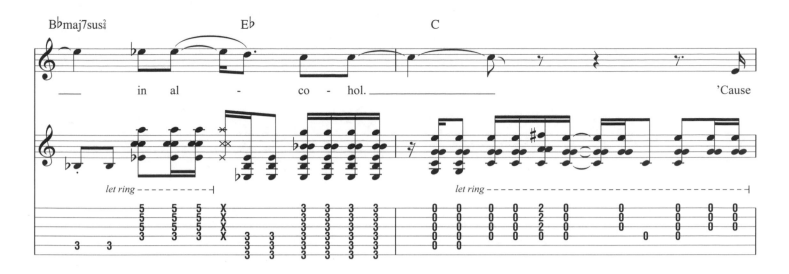

in al - co - hol. _____ 'Cause

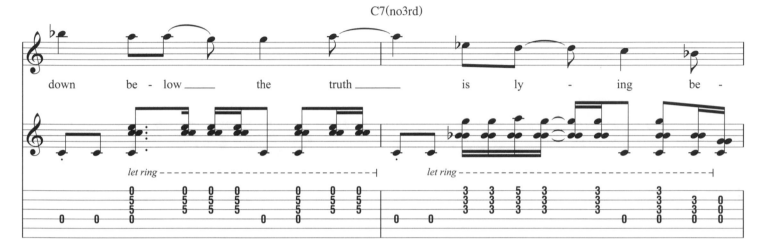

down be - low _____ the truth _____ is ly - ing be -

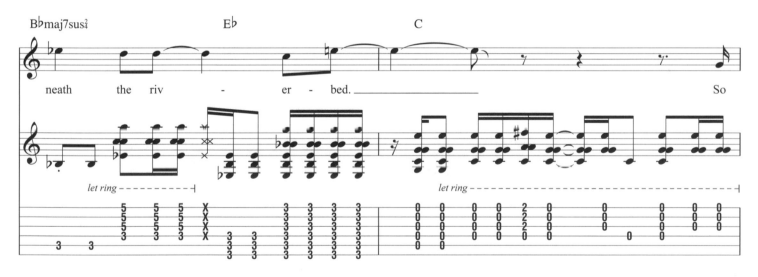

neath the riv - er - bed. _____ So

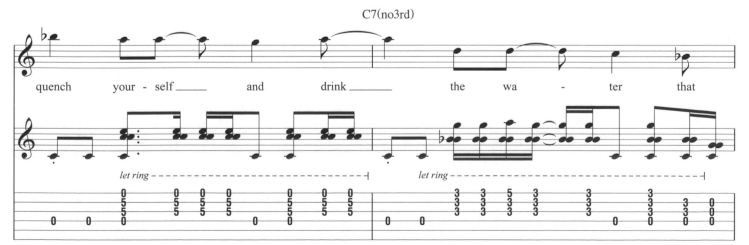

quench your - self _____ and drink _____ the wa - ter that

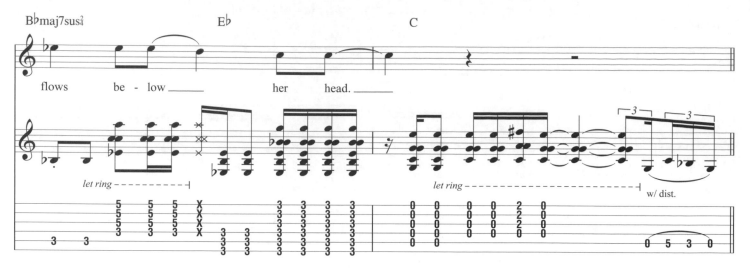

Pre-Chorus

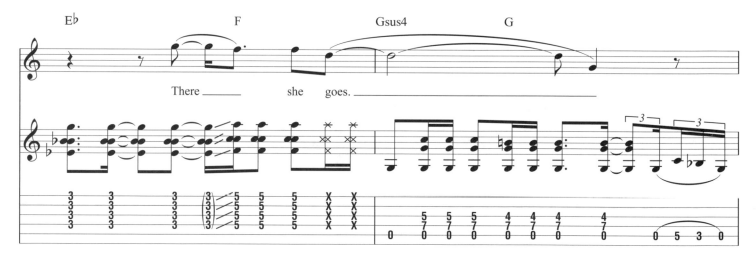

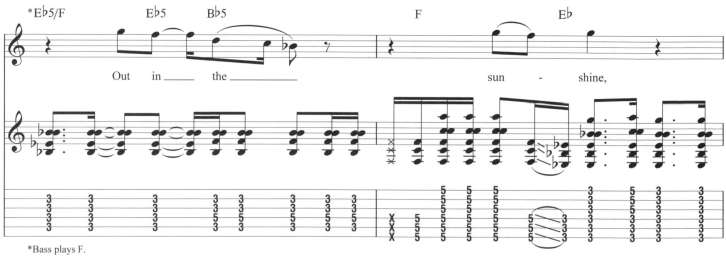

*Bass plays F.

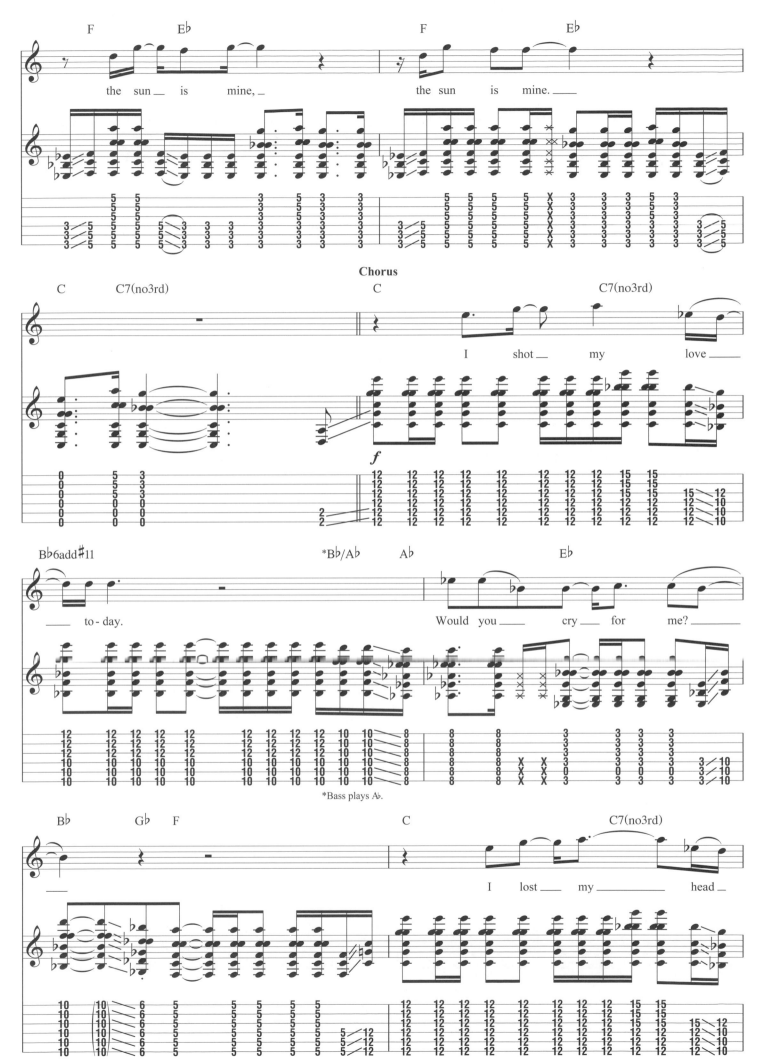

the sun __ is mine, __ the sun is mine. __

I shot __ my love __

__ to - day. Would you __ cry __ for me? __

I lost __ my __ head __

*Bass plays A♭.

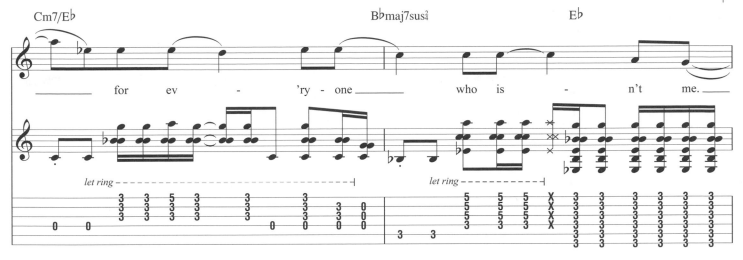

for ev - 'ry - one _____ who is - n't me. _____

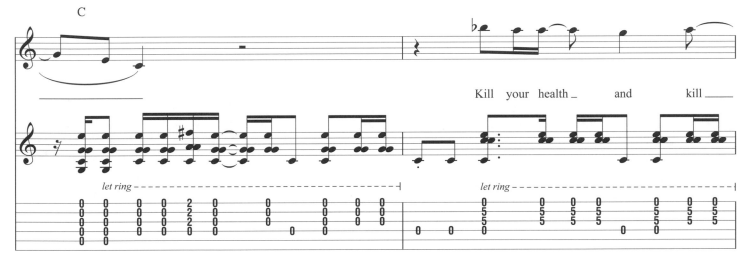

Kill your health _____ and kill _____

your - self _____ and kill ev - 'ry - thing _____ you love.

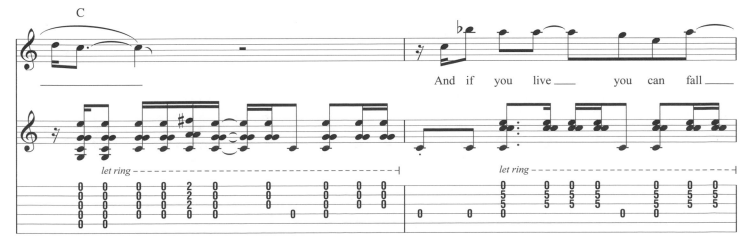

And if you live _____ you can fall _____

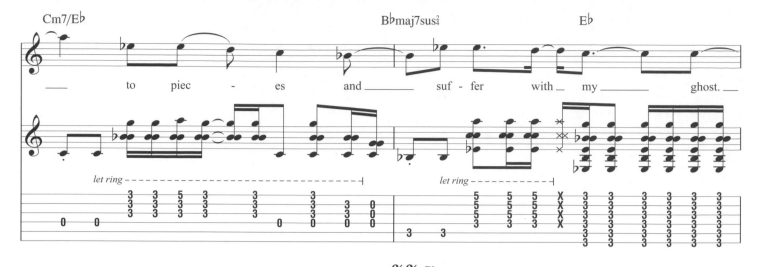

to piec - es and suf - fer with my ghost.

Chorus

I shot my love

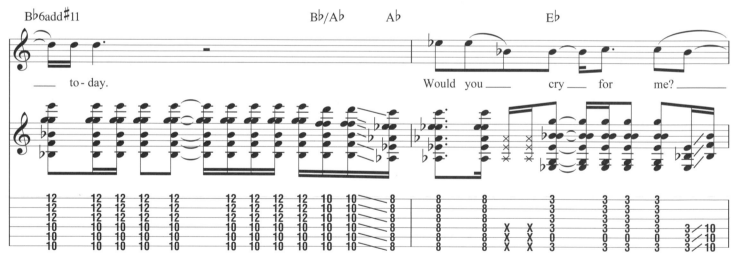

to - day. Would you cry for me?

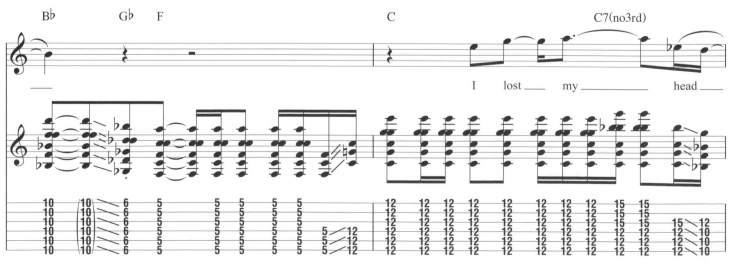

I lost my head

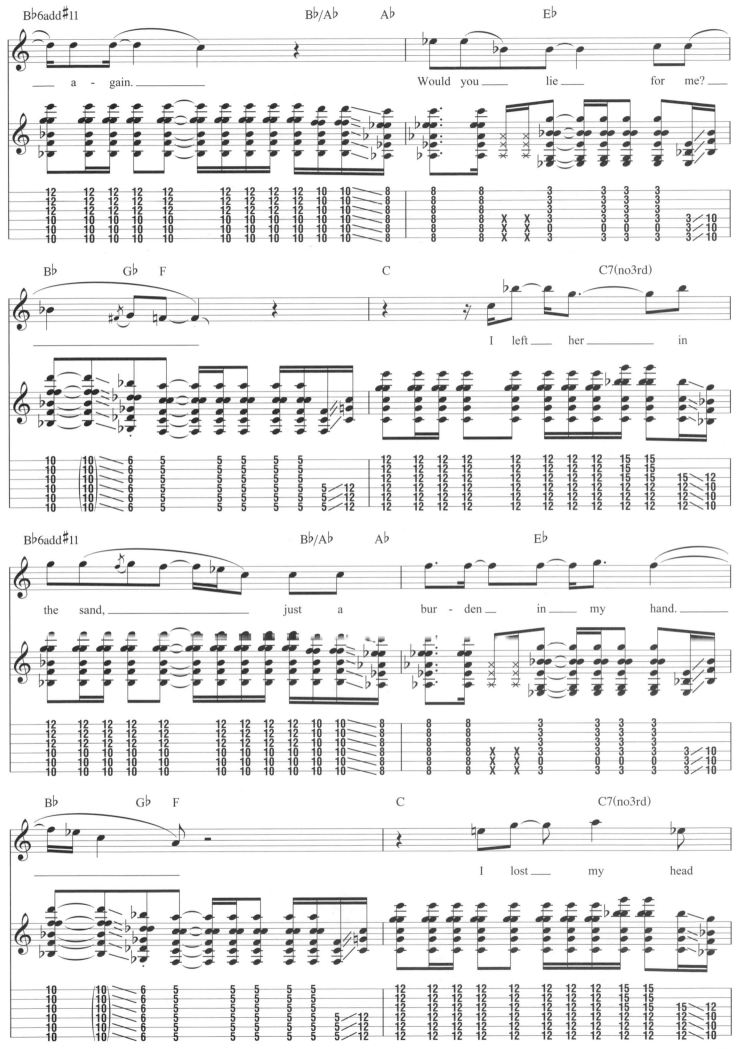

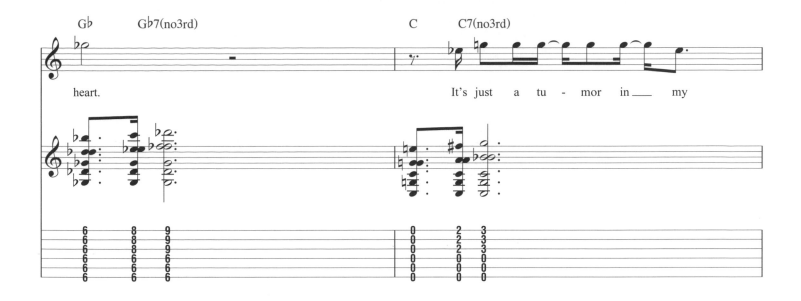

heart.   It's just a tu - mor in ___ my

D.S. al Coda 1

head,   and I'm in   the   dark. ___   3. So

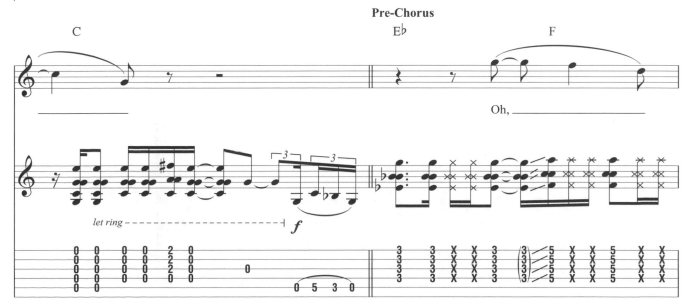

Coda 1

Pre-Chorus

Oh, _____

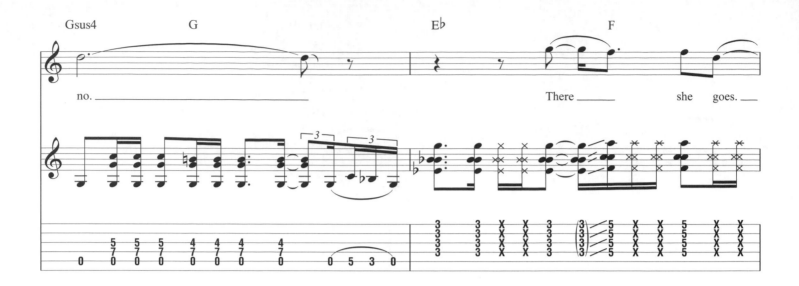

no. _____   There _____ she goes. ___

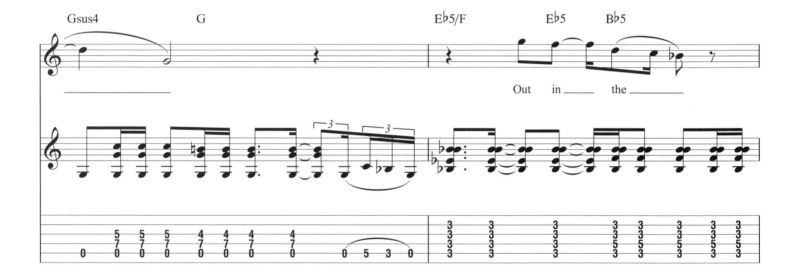

_____   Out in _____ the _____

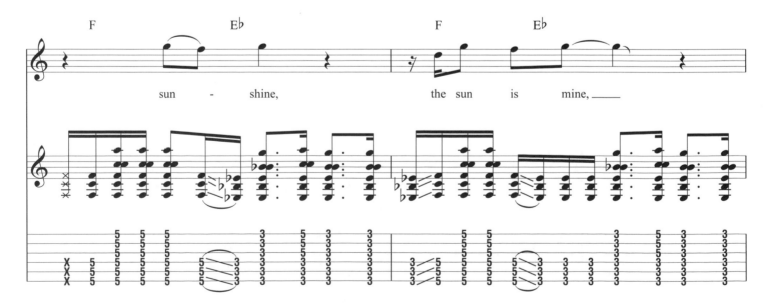

sun - shine,   the sun is mine, _____

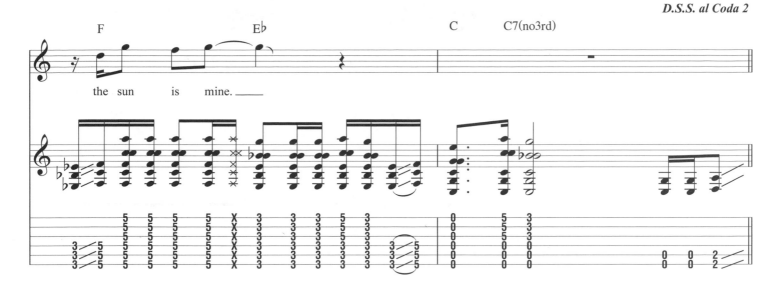

Coda 2

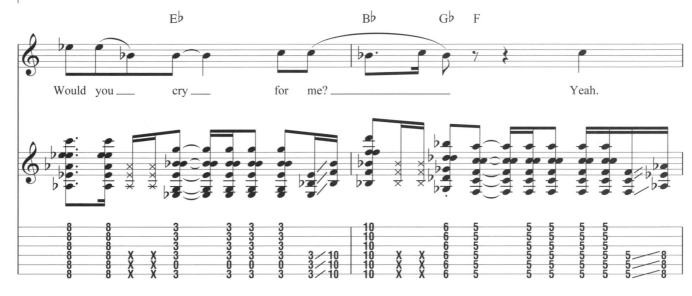

Additional Lyrics

3. So follow me into the desert, as desp'rate as you are,
   Where the moon is glued to a picture of heaven and all the little pigs have God.

Jesus Christ Pose

Words by Chris Cornell
Music by Chris Cornell, Matt Cameron, Hunter Shepherd and Kim Thayil

Drop D tuning:
(low to high) D-A-D-G-B-E

Intro
Moderately fast Rock ♩ = 135

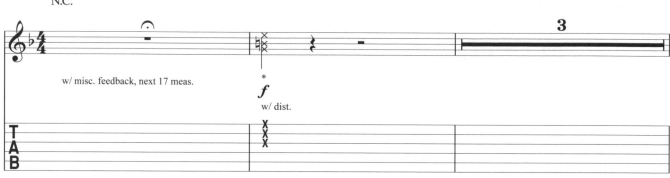

*Pluck strings behind nut.

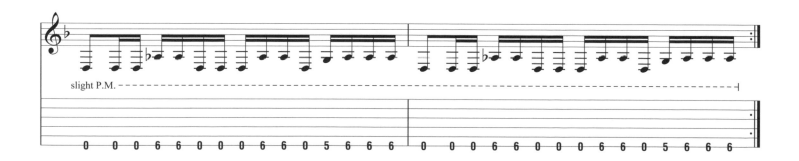

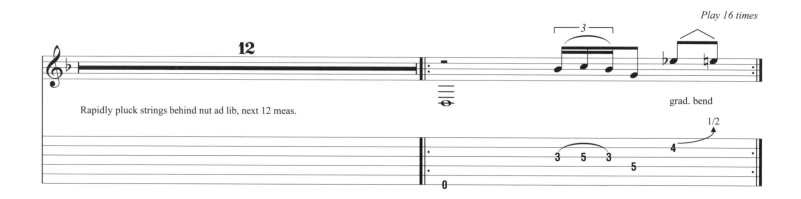

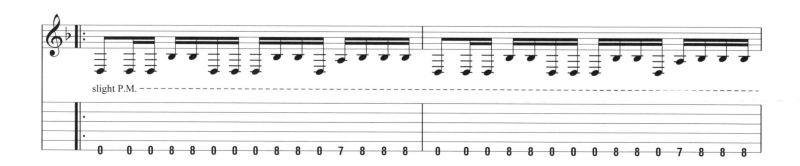

1. And you

Verse

N.C.

stare   at _____   me _____   in   your
2. *See additional lyrics*

slight P.M. ‑

Je - sus _____ Christ _____   pose, _____

slight P.M. ‑

arms   held _____   out _____   like   you've   been

slight P.M. ‑

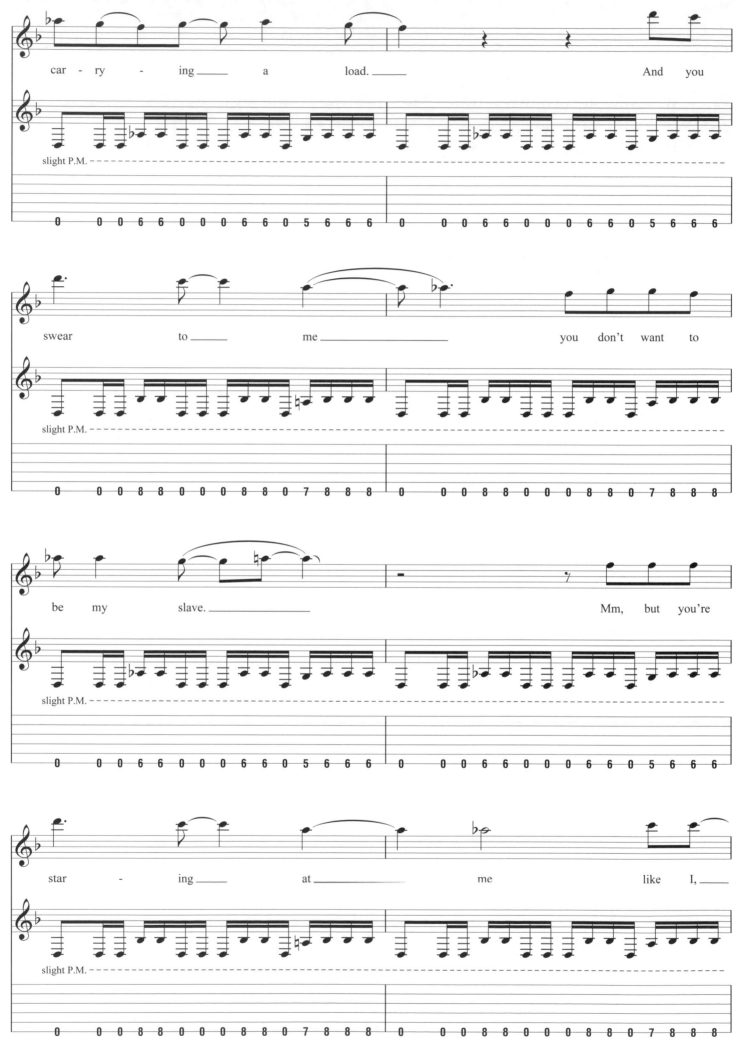

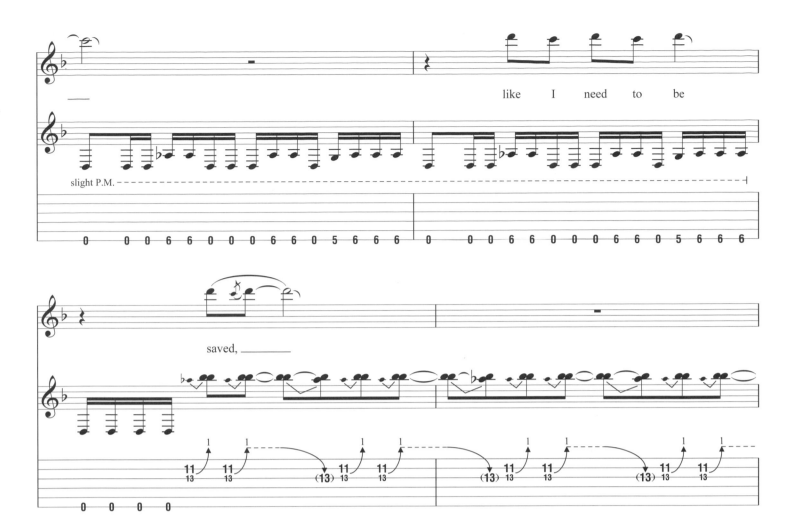

like I need to be

slight P.M. --

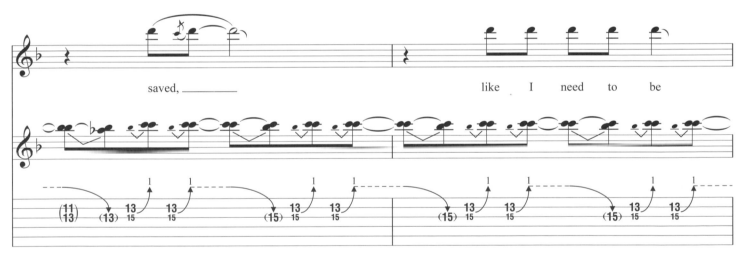

saved, _____

saved, _____

like I need to be

To Coda ⊕

saved, _____

saved. _____ In your

Chorus

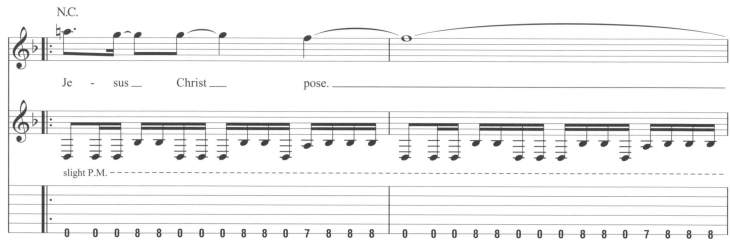

Je - sus __ Christ __ pose. _____

slight P.M. -

1.

_____ In your

slight P.M. -

2.

Interlude

N.C.

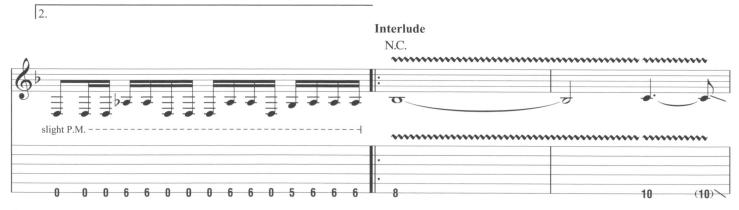

slight P.M. -

⊕ Coda

nails, _____

like I'm driv - ing the   nails, _____

nails, _____   nails, _____

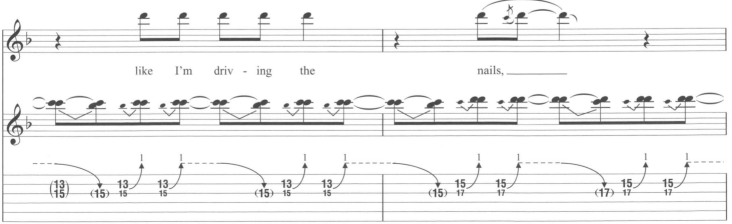

like I'm driv - ing the   nails, _____

nails.

Chorus

D5

In your Je - sus Christ pose.

C5   D5

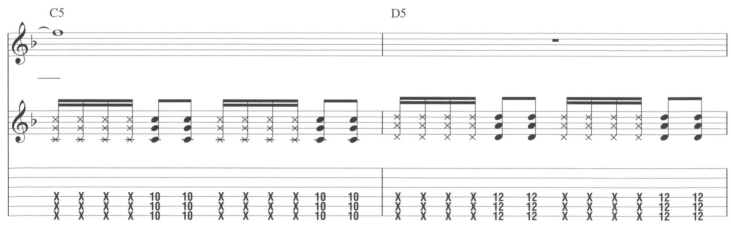

1.   2.

C5   C5

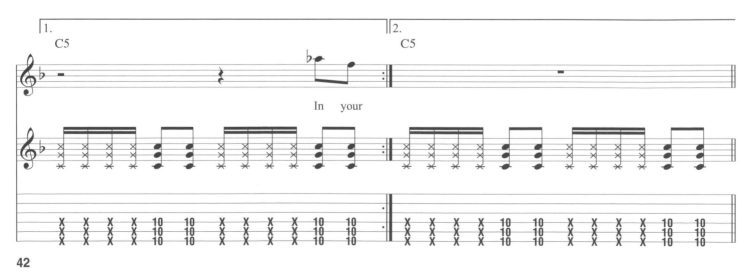

In your

Interlude

Verse

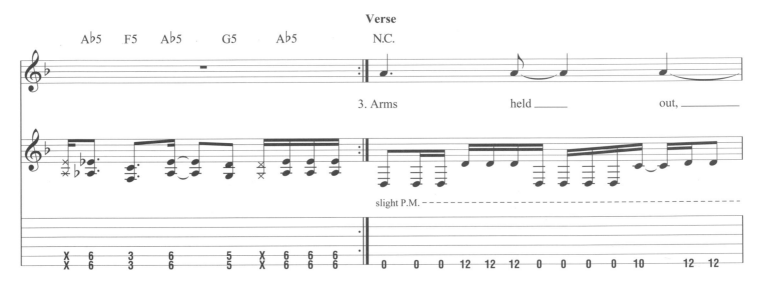

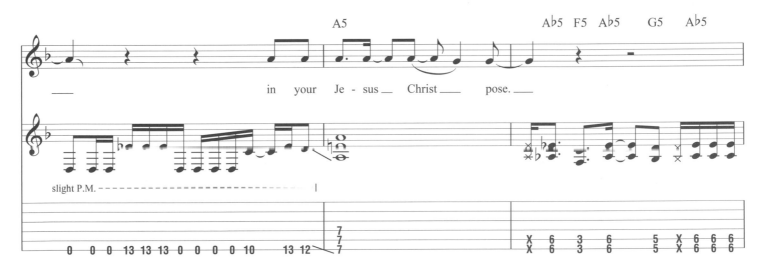

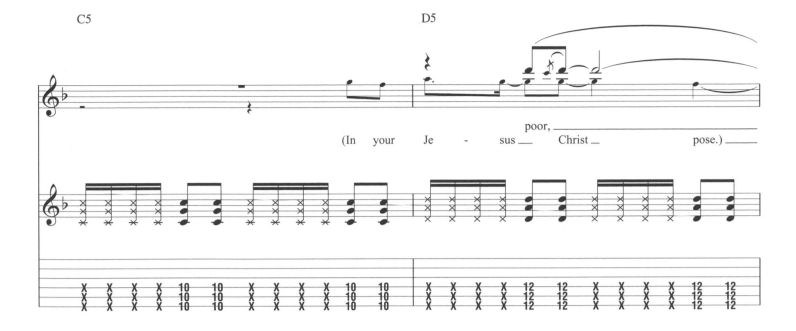

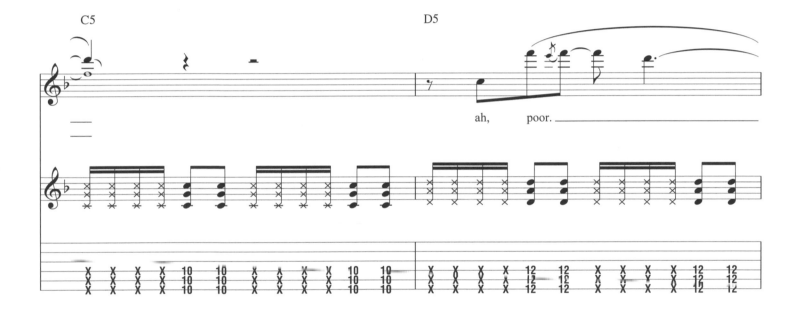

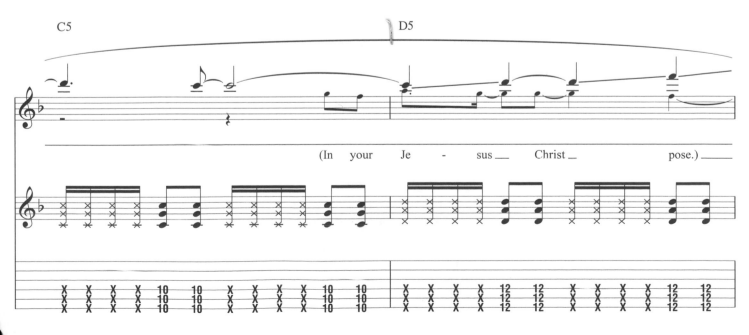

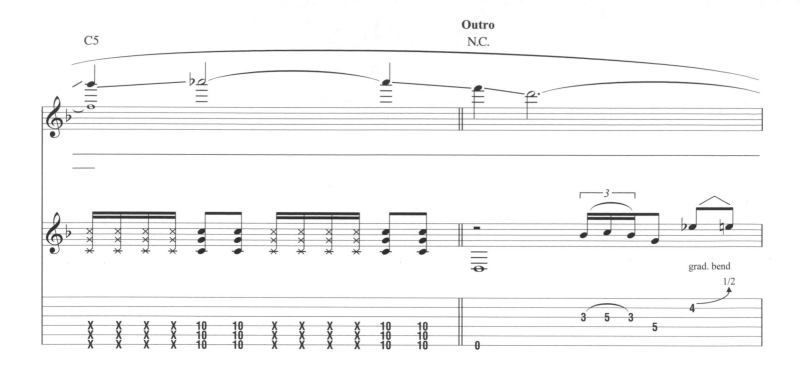

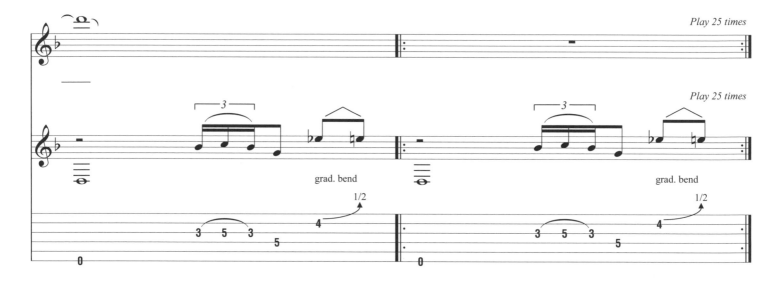

Free time

Additional Lyrics

2. Arms held out in your Jesus Christ pose.
   Thorns and shroud, like it's the coming of the Lord.
   And I swear to you I would never feed you pain.
   Mm, but you're staring at me like I'm,
   Like I'm driving the nails, nails,
   Like I'm driving the nails, nails,
   Like I'm driving the nails, nails, nails,
   Like I'm driving the nails, nails.

Outshined

Words and Music by Chris Cornell

kept the mov-ie roll - in', __ but the sto-ry's get-ting old now. __ Oh __

2nd time, substitute Fill 1

yeah. __ Well, I just looked in the mir - ror, __ and

things aren't look-in' so good. _____ I'm look-in' Cal-i-for - nia __ and

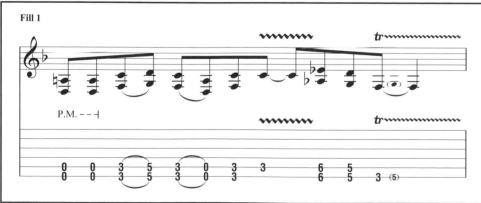

Fill 1

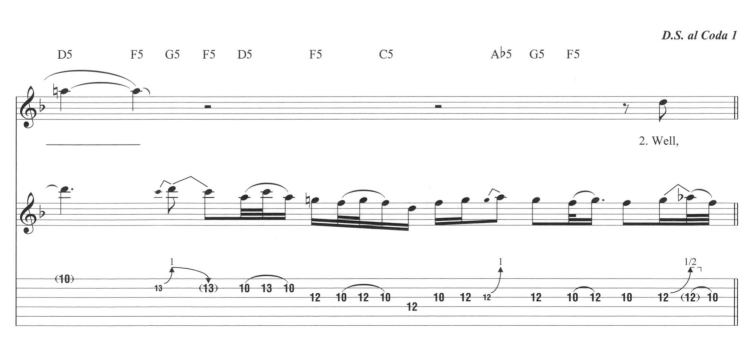

Coda 1

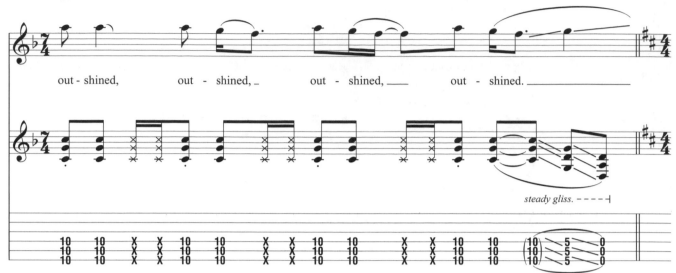

out - shined, out - shined, _ out - shined, ____ out - shined. _____

Interlude

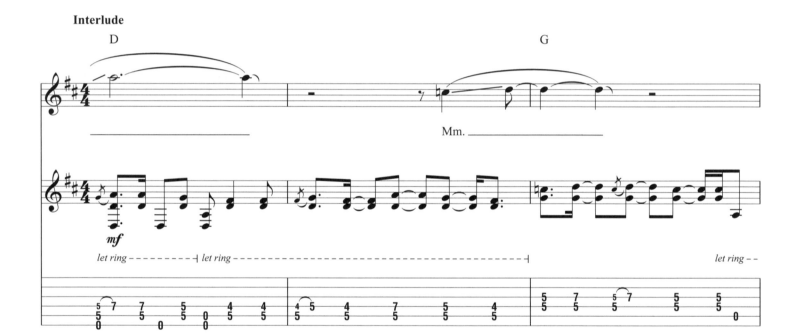

Mm. _____

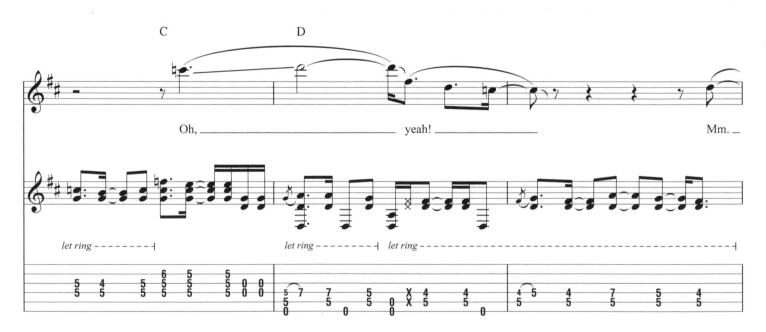

Oh, _____ yeah! _____ Mm. _

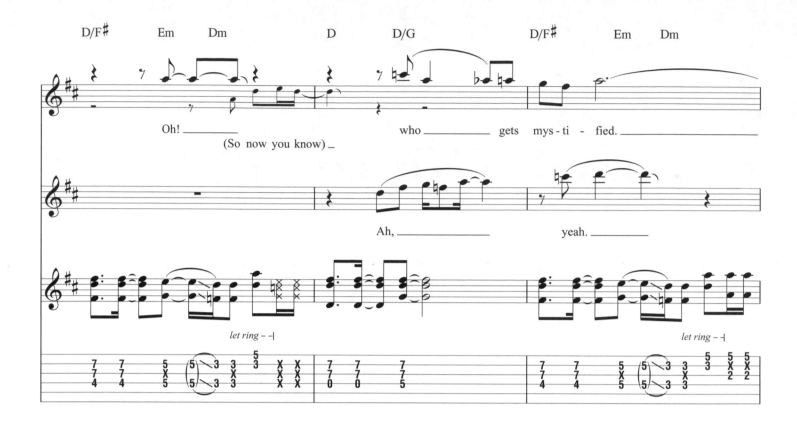

Oh! ____

(So now you know) ____

who ____ gets mys-ti-fied. ____

Ah, ____ yeah. ____

let ring ───┤

let ring ───┤

D.S.S. al Coda 2   **Coda 2**

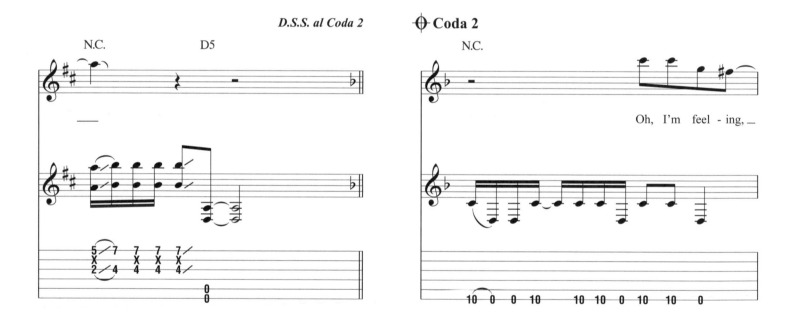

____

Oh, I'm feel-ing, ____

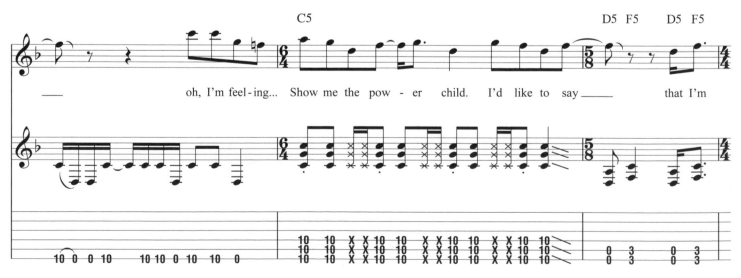

____ oh, I'm feel-ing... Show me the pow-er child. I'd like to say ____ that I'm

Additional Lyrics

2. Well, someone let the dogs out.
They'll show you where the truth is.
The grass is always greener
Where the dogs are shitting. Oh, yeah.
Well, I'm feeling that I'm sober,
Even though I'm drinking.
But I can't get any lower.
Still I feel I'm sinking.

My Wave

Words and Music by Chris Cornell and Kim Thayil

Tuning:
(low to high) E-E↓-B↓-B↑-B-B↓

Intro
Moderately fast ♩ = 126

G5 A5 N.C. G5 A5 N.C. G5 A5

Play 3 times

f

w/ dist.

E5 G5 A5 E5 G5 A5 E5 G5 A5

Yeah. —

E5 G5 A5 E5 G5 A5 E5 G5 A5

Play 3 times

Chorus

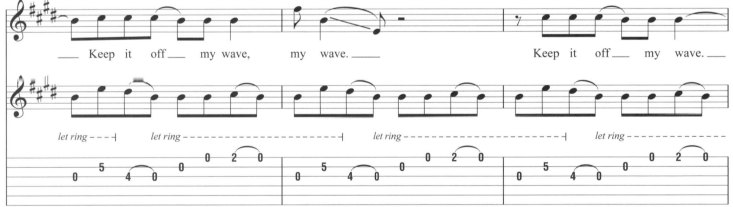

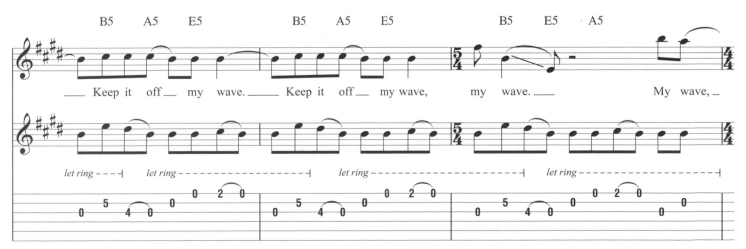

To Coda 2 ⊕

my wave, ___ my wave, ___ my wave, ___ my wave. _____

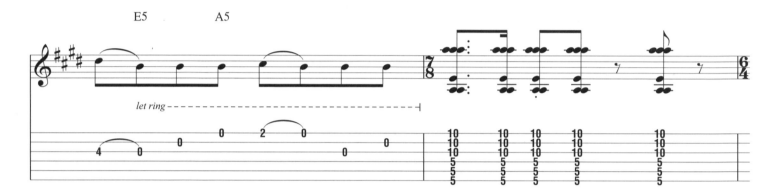

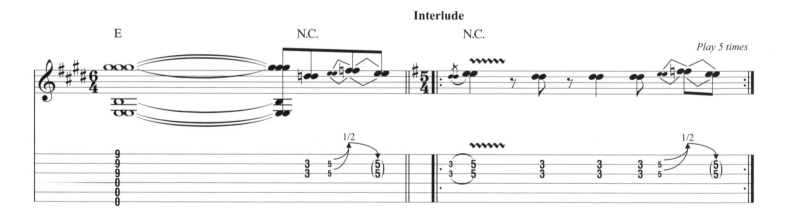

Interlude

Play 5 times

Verse

3. Cry ___ if ___ you wan - na cry, if ___ it helps ___ you see, if ___ it clears ___ your

my wave, __ my wave, __ my wave, __ my wave. __ Keep

it off __ my wave. Keep it off __ my wave, __ my wave. __

Outro

Keep it off __ my wave. __

*Chords implied by bass till end.

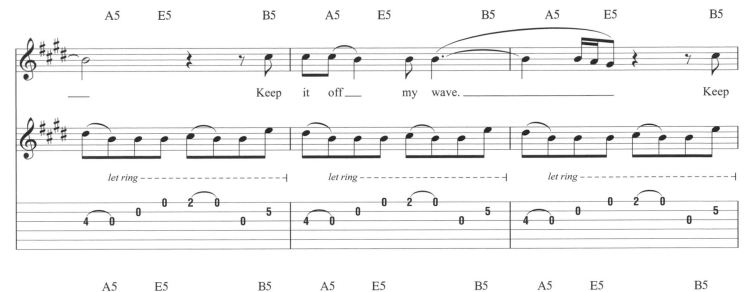

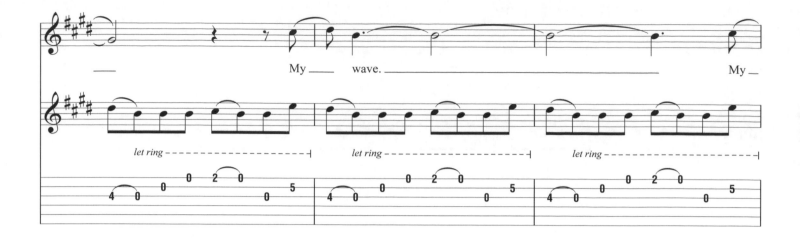

My ___ wave. _____ My ___

___ wave. _____

Keep it off _____ my _____ wave. _____

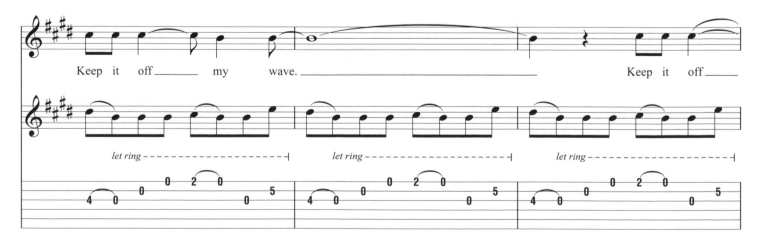

Keep it off _____ my ____ wave. _____ Keep it off _____

my wave.

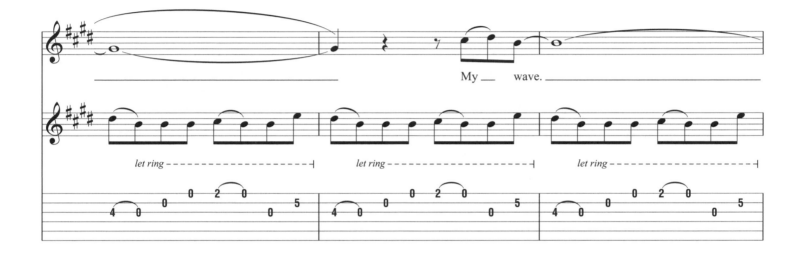

My __ wave.

Additional Lyrics

2. Cry if you wanna cry, if it helps you see, if it clears your eyes.
   Hate if you wanna hate, if it keeps you safe, if it makes you brave.
   Pray if you wanna pray, if you like to kneel, if you like to lay.
   Don't come over here, piss on my gate.
   Save it, just keep it off my wave.

Rusty Cage

Words and Music by Chris Cornell

Tuning:
(low to high) B↓-A-D-G-B-E

Intro
Very fast Rock ♩ = 204

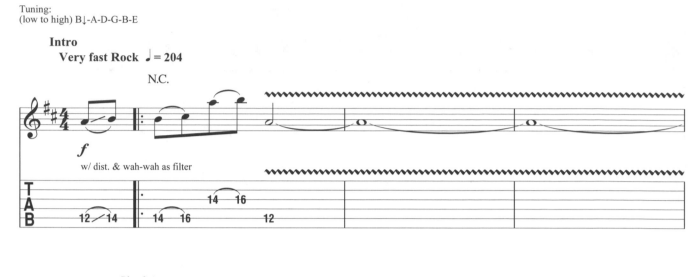

1. Oh, _____ you wi - red me a - wake and
2. *See additional lyrics*

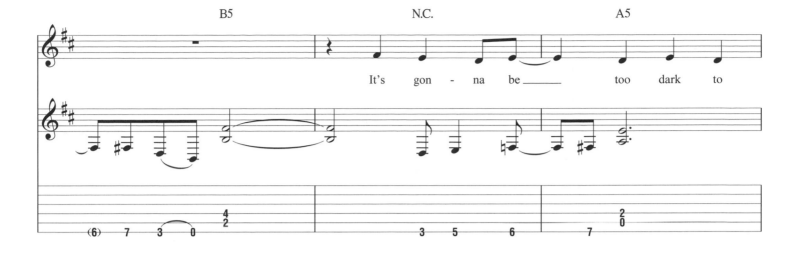

It's gon-na be ____ too dark to

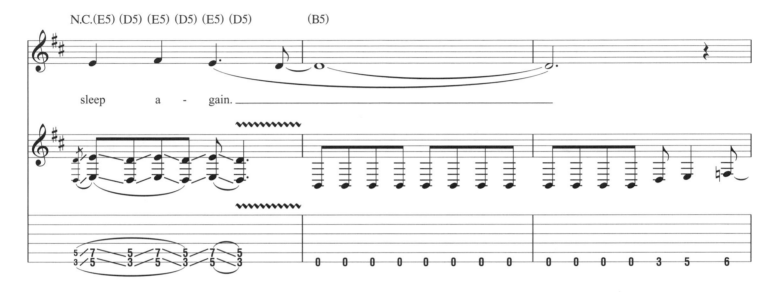

sleep a-gain. ____

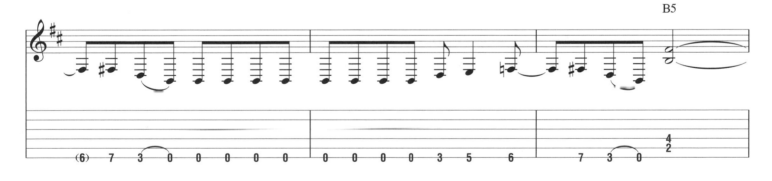

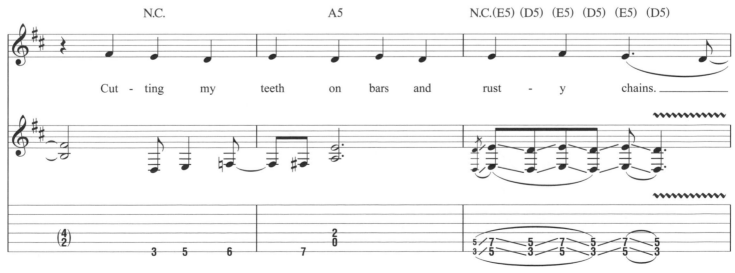

Cut-ting my teeth on bars and rust-y chains. ____

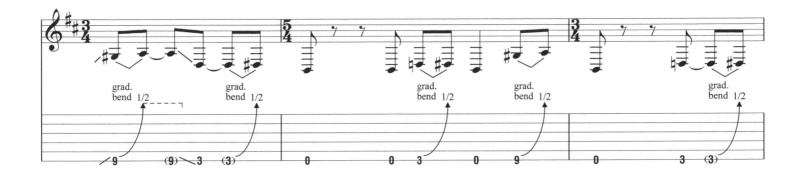

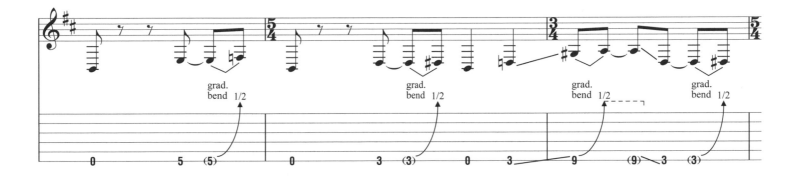

Outro

N.C.

When the   for - est burns_ a - long   the   road, _____

_____   like

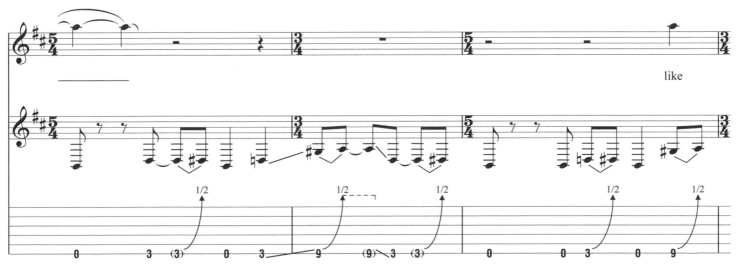

God's eyes _____ in my head - lights, _____

and when the dogs are look - ing

for their bones, _____

and it's rain - ing ice - picks ____ on your steel

Additional Lyrics

2. Too cold to start a fire, I'm burning diesel, burning dinosaur bones.
Yeah, I'll take the river down to still water and ride a pack of dogs.
But I'm gonna break, I'm gonna break my...
I'm gonna break my rusty cage and run.
Yeah, I'm gonna break, I'm gonna break my...
I'm gonna break my rusty cage and run.

Spoonman

Words and Music by Chris Cornell

Drop D tuning:
(low to high) D-A-D-G-B-E

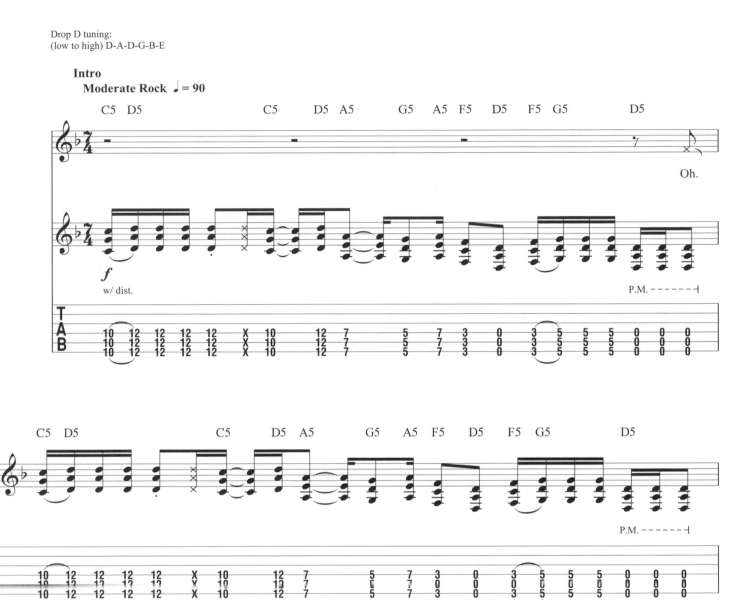

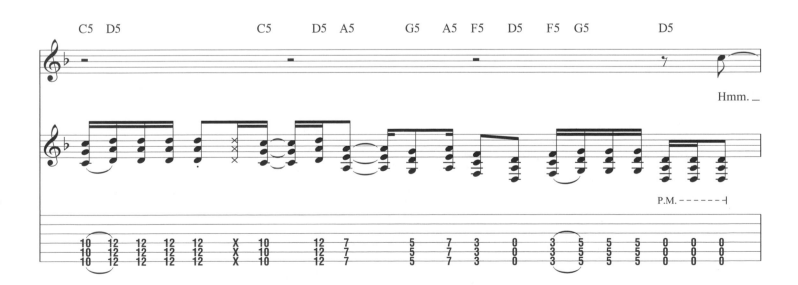

Verse

feel __ the rhy - thm   with __ your   hands. ____

2. See additional lyrics

Steal   the   rhy - thm   while   you   can.

Spoon - man. ____

Ah,

save, _____

ah, with your...

Interlude
Gtr. tacet
N.C.

Come on, come on, _____ come on. Come on, come on, _____ come on.

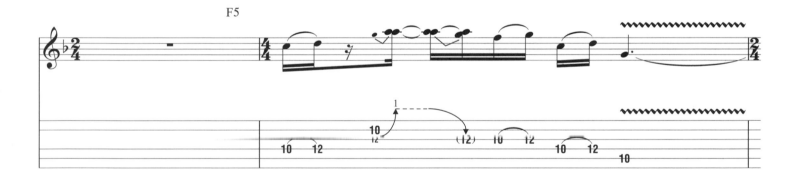

Ah, with your

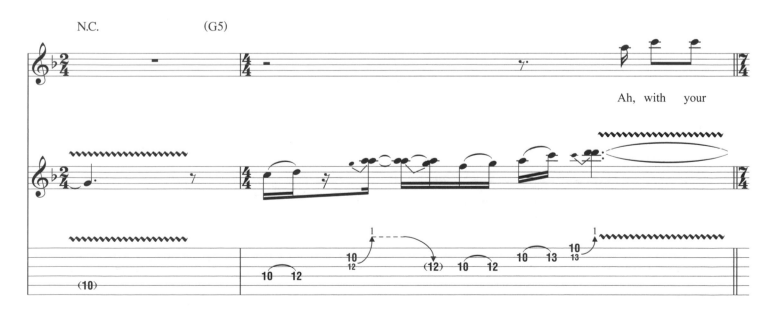

Guitar Solo

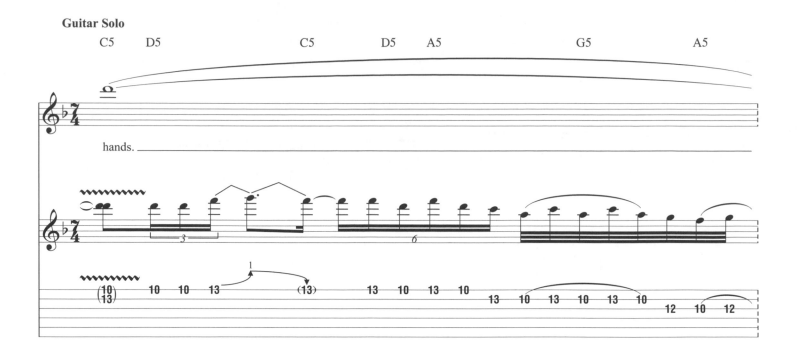

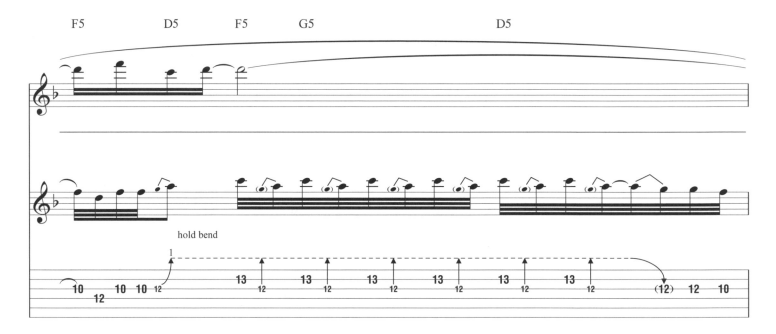

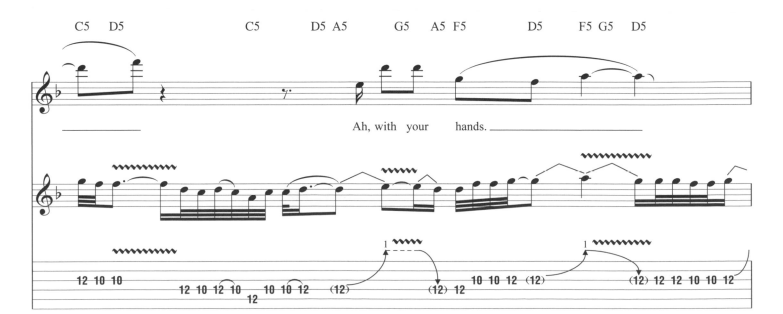

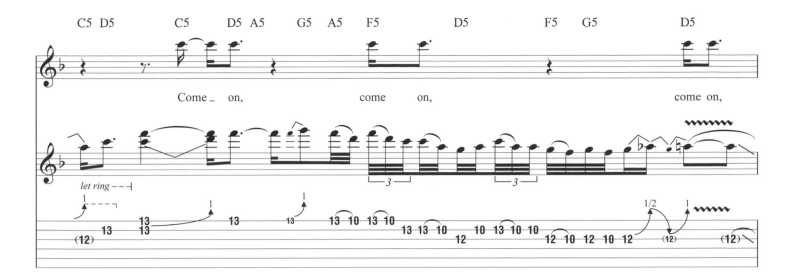

Come on, come on, come on,

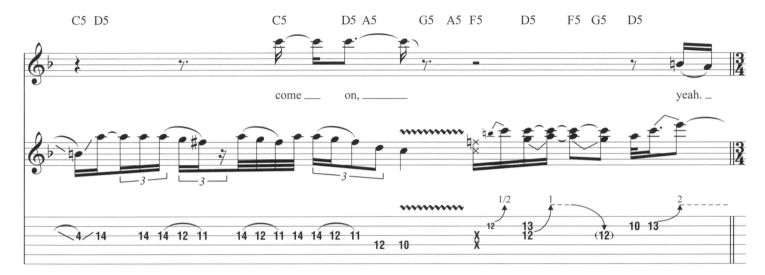

come on, yeah.

Interlude
N.C.

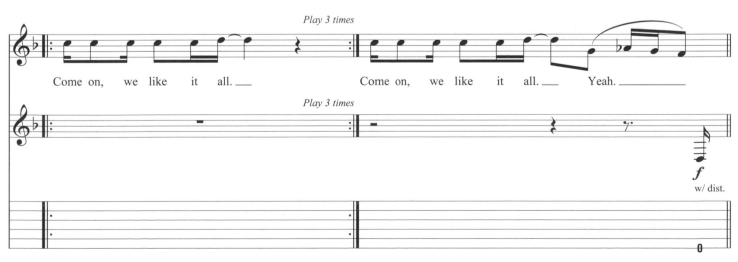

Come on, we like it all. Come on, we like it all. Yeah.

Come on, we like it all. __ Come on, we like it all. __

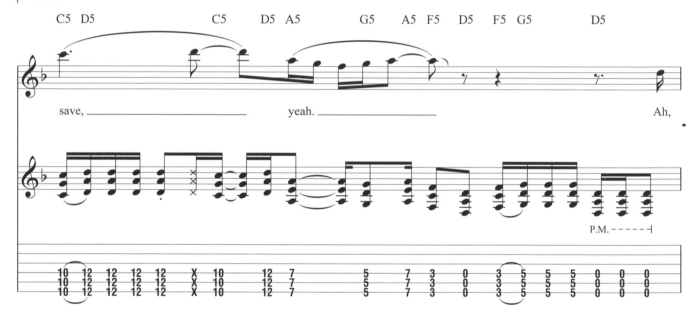

Coda

save, _____ yeah. _____ Ah,

save me, _____ yeah. Ah, with your,

Additional Lyrics

2. Well, all my friends are Indians.
   All my friends are brown and red.
   Spoonman.
   And all my friends are skeletons,
   And they beat the rhythms with their bones.
   Spoonman. Oh, hmm.

Chorus 2. Spoonman, ah, come together with your hands.
   Save me. I'm together with your plan.
   Save me, yeah.
   Ah, save, ah, save me.
   Save me, yeah.
   Save, ah, with your...

Chorus 3. Spoonman, come together with your hands.
   Save me. I'm together with your plan.
   Save me, yeah.
   Ah, save, yeah.
   Ah, save me, yeah.
   Ah, with your, ah, with your hands.
   Feel the rhythm with your hands.
   Steal the rhythm while you can.
   Spoonman.

GUITAR RECORDED VERSIONS®

Guitar Recorded Versions® are note-for-note transcriptions of guitar music taken directly off recordings. This series, one of the most popular in print today, features some of the greatest guitar players and groups from blues and rock to country and jazz.

Guitar Recorded Versions are transcribed by the best transcribers in the business. Every book contains notes and tablature. Visit **www.halleonard.com** for our complete selection.

**AUTHENTIC TRANSCRIPTIONS
WITH NOTES AND TABLATURE**

HAL•LEONARD® CORPORATION

7777 W. BLUEMOUND RD. P.O. BOX 13819 MILWAUKEE, WI 53213

Complete songlists and more at **www.halleonard.com**

Prices, contents, and availability subject to change without notice.

0515

HAL•LEONARD GUITAR PLAY-ALONG

This series will help you play your favorite songs quickly and easily. Just follow the tab and listen to the CD to the hear how the guitar should sound, and then play along using the separate backing tracks. Mac or PC users can also slow down the tempo without changing pitch by using the CD in their computer. The melody and lyrics are included in the book so that you can sing or simply follow along.

INCLUDES TAB

VOL. 1 – ROCK	00699570 / $16.99	**VOL. 59 – CHET ATKINS**	00702347 / $16.99	**VOL. 119 – AC/DC CLASSICS**	00701356 / $17.99

VOL. 1 – ROCK — 00699570 / $16.99
VOL. 2 – ACOUSTIC — 00699569 / $16.95
VOL. 3 – HARD ROCK — 00699573 / $16.95
VOL. 4 – POP/ROCK — 00699571 / $16.99
VOL. 5 – MODERN ROCK — 00699574 / $16.99
VOL. 6 – '90S ROCK — 00699572 / $16.99
VOL. 7 – BLUES — 00699575 / $16.95
VOL. 8 – ROCK — 00699585 / $14.99
VOL. 9 – PUNK ROCK — 00699576 / $14.95
VOL. 10 – ACOUSTIC — 00699586 / $16.95
VOL. 11 – EARLY ROCK — 00699579 / $14.95
VOL. 12 – POP/ROCK — 00699587 / $14.95
VOL. 13 – FOLK ROCK — 00699581 / $15.99
VOL. 14 – BLUES ROCK — 00699582 / $16.95
VOL. 15 – R&B — 00699583 / $14.95
VOL. 16 – JAZZ — 00699584 / $15.95
VOL. 17 – COUNTRY — 00699588 / $15.95
VOL. 18 – ACOUSTIC ROCK — 00699577 / $15.95
VOL. 19 – SOUL — 00699578 / $14.99
VOL. 20 – ROCKABILLY — 00699580 / $14.95
VOL. 21 – YULETIDE — 00699602 / $14.95
VOL. 22 – CHRISTMAS — 00699600 / $15.95
VOL. 23 – SURF — 00699635 / $14.95
VOL. 24 – ERIC CLAPTON — 00699649 / $17.99
VOL. 25 – LENNON & MCCARTNEY — 00699642 / $16.99
VOL. 26 – ELVIS PRESLEY — 00699643 / $14.95
VOL. 27 – DAVID LEE ROTH — 00699645 / $16.95
VOL. 28 – GREG KOCH — 00699646 / $14.95
VOL. 29 – BOB SEGER — 00699647 / $15.99
VOL. 30 – KISS — 00699644 / $16.99
VOL. 31 – CHRISTMAS HITS — 00699652 / $14.95
VOL. 32 – THE OFFSPRING — 00699653 / $14.95
VOL. 33 – ACOUSTIC CLASSICS — 00699656 / $16.95
VOL. 34 – CLASSIC ROCK — 00699658 / $16.95
VOL. 35 – HAIR METAL — 00699660 / $16.95
VOL. 36 – SOUTHERN ROCK — 00699661 / $16.95
VOL. 37 – ACOUSTIC UNPLUGGED — 00699662 / $22.99
VOL. 38 – BLUES — 00699663 / $16.95
VOL. 39 – '80S METAL — 00699664 / $16.99
VOL. 40 – INCUBUS — 00699668 / $17.95
VOL. 41 – ERIC CLAPTON — 00699669 / $16.95
VOL. 42 – 2000S ROCK — 00699670 / $16.99
VOL. 43 – LYNYRD SKYNYRD — 00699681 / $17.95
VOL. 44 – JAZZ — 00699689 / $14.99
VOL. 45 – TV THEMES — 00699718 / $14.95
VOL. 46 – MAINSTREAM ROCK — 00699722 / $16.95
VOL. 47 – HENDRIX SMASH HITS — 00699723 / $19.95
VOL. 48 – AEROSMITH CLASSICS — 00699724 / $17.99
VOL. 49 – STEVIE RAY VAUGHAN — 00699725 / $17.99
VOL. 51 – ALTERNATIVE '90S — 00699727 / $14.99
VOL. 52 – FUNK — 00699728 / $14.95
VOL. 53 – DISCO — 00699729 / $14.99
VOL. 54 – HEAVY METAL — 00699730 / $14.95
VOL. 55 – POP METAL — 00699731 / $14.95
VOL. 56 – FOO FIGHTERS — 00699749 / $15.99
VOL. 57 – SYSTEM OF A DOWN — 00699751 / $14.95
VOL. 58 – BLINK-182 — 00699772 / $14.95

VOL. 59 – CHET ATKINS — 00702347 / $16.99
VOL. 60 – 3 DOORS DOWN — 00699774 / $14.95
VOL. 61 – SLIPKNOT — 00699775 / $16.99
VOL. 62 – CHRISTMAS CAROLS — 00699798 / $12.95
VOL. 63 – CREEDENCE CLEARWATER REVIVAL — 00699802 / $16.99
VOL. 64 – THE ULTIMATE OZZY OSBOURNE — 00699803 / $16.99
VOL. 66 – THE ROLLING STONES — 00699807 / $16.95
VOL. 67 – BLACK SABBATH — 00699808 / $16.99
VOL. 68 – PINK FLOYD – DARK SIDE OF THE MOON — 00699809 / $16.99
VOL. 69 – ACOUSTIC FAVORITES — 00699810 / $14.95
VOL. 70 – OZZY OSBOURNE — 00699805 / $16.99
VOL. 71 – CHRISTIAN ROCK — 00699824 / $14.95
VOL. 73 – BLUESY ROCK — 00699829 / $16.99
VOL. 75 – TOM PETTY — 00699882 / $16.99
VOL. 76 – COUNTRY HITS — 00699884 / $14.95
VOL. 77 – BLUEGRASS — 00699910 / $14.99
VOL. 78 – NIRVANA — 00700132 / $16.99
VOL. 79 – NEIL YOUNG — 00700133 / $24.99
VOL. 80 – ACOUSTIC ANTHOLOGY — 00700175 / $19.95
VOL. 81 – ROCK ANTHOLOGY — 00700176 / $22.99
VOL. 82 – EASY SONGS — 00700177 / $12.99
VOL. 83 – THREE CHORD SONGS — 00700178 / $16.99
VOL. 84 – STEELY DAN — 00700200 / $16.99
VOL. 85 – THE POLICE — 00700269 / $16.99
VOL. 86 – BOSTON — 00700465 / $16.99
VOL. 87 – ACOUSTIC WOMEN — 00700763 / $14.99
VOL. 88 – GRUNGE — 00700467 / $16.99
VOL. 89 – REGGAE — 00700468 / $15.99
VOL. 90 – CLASSICAL POP — 00700469 / $14.99
VOL. 91 – BLUES INSTRUMENTALS — 00700505 / $14.99
VOL. 92 – EARLY ROCK INSTRUMENTALS — 00700506 / $14.99
VOL. 93 – ROCK INSTRUMENTALS — 00700507 / $16.99
VOL. 95 – BLUES CLASSICS — 00700509 / $14.99
VOL. 96 – THIRD DAY — 00700560 / $14.95
VOL. 97 – ROCK BAND — 00700703 / $14.99
VOL. 99 – ZZ TOP — 00700762 / $16.99
VOL. 100 – B.B. KING — 00700466 / $16.99
VOL. 101 – SONGS FOR BEGINNERS — 00701917 / $14.99
VOL. 102 – CLASSIC PUNK — 00700769 / $14.99
VOL. 103 – SWITCHFOOT — 00700773 / $16.99
VOL. 104 – DUANE ALLMAN — 00700846 / $16.99
VOL. 106 – WEEZER — 00700958 / $14.99
VOL. 107 – CREAM — 00701069 / $16.99
VOL. 108 – THE WHO — 00701053 / $16.99
VOL. 109 – STEVE MILLER — 00701054 / $14.99
VOL. 111 – JOHN MELLENCAMP — 00701056 / $14.99
VOL. 112 – QUEEN — 00701052 / $16.99
VOL. 113 – JIM CROCE — 00701058 / $15.99
VOL. 114 – BON JOVI — 00701060 / $14.99
VOL. 115 – JOHNNY CASH — 00701070 / $16.99
VOL. 116 – THE VENTURES — 00701124 / $14.99
VOL. 117 – BRAD PAISLEY — 00701224 / $16.99
VOL. 118 – ERIC JOHNSON — 00701353 / $16.99

VOL. 119 – AC/DC CLASSICS — 00701356 / $17.99
VOL. 120 – PROGRESSIVE ROCK — 00701457 / $14.99
VOL. 121 – U2 — 00701508 / $16.99
VOL. 123 – LENNON & MCCARTNEY ACOUSTIC — 00701614 / $16.99
VOL. 124 – MODERN WORSHIP — 00701629 / $14.99
VOL. 125 – JEFF BECK — 00701687 / $16.99
VOL. 126 – BOB MARLEY — 00701701 / $16.99
VOL. 127 – 1970S ROCK — 00701739 / $14.99
VOL. 128 – 1960S ROCK — 00701740 / $14.99
VOL. 129 – MEGADETH — 00701741 / $16.99
VOL. 131 – 1990S ROCK — 00701743 / $14.99
VOL. 132 – COUNTRY ROCK — 00701757 / $15.99
VOL. 133 – TAYLOR SWIFT — 00701894 / $16.99
VOL. 134 – AVENGED SEVENFOLD — 00701906 / $16.99
VOL. 136 – GUITAR THEMES — 00701922 / $14.99
VOL. 137 – IRISH TUNES — 00701966 / $15.99
VOL. 138 – BLUEGRASS CLASSICS — 00701967 / $14.99
VOL. 139 – GARY MOORE — 00702370 / $16.99
VOL. 140 – MORE STEVIE RAY VAUGHAN — 00702396 / $17.99
VOL. 141 – ACOUSTIC HITS — 00702401 / $16.99
VOL. 142 – KINGS OF LEON — 00702418 / $16.99
VOL. 144 – DJANGO REINHARDT — 00702531 / $16.99
VOL. 145 – DEF LEPPARD — 00702532 / $16.99
VOL. 147 – SIMON & GARFUNKEL — 14041591 / $16.99
VOL. 148 – BOB DYLAN — 14041592 / $16.99
VOL. 149 – AC/DC HITS — 14041593 / $17.99
VOL. 150 – ZAKK WYLDE — 02501717 / $16.99
VOL. 153 – RED HOT CHILI PEPPERS — 00702990 / $19.99
VOL. 156 – SLAYER — 00703770 / $17.99
VOL. 157 – FLEETWOOD MAC — 00101382 / $16.99
VOL. 158 – ULTIMATE CHRISTMAS — 00101889 / $14.99
VOL. 160 – T-BONE WALKER — 00102641 / $16.99
VOL. 161 – THE EAGLES – ACOUSTIC — 00102659 / $17.99
VOL. 162 – THE EAGLES HITS — 00102667 / $17.99
VOL. 163 – PANTERA — 00103036 / $17.99
VOL. 166 – MODERN BLUES — 00700764 / $16.99
VOL. 168 – KISS — 00113421 / $16.99
VOL. 169 – TAYLOR SWIFT — 00115982 / $16.99
VOL. 170 – THREE DAYS GRACE — 00117337 / $16.99
VOL. 172 – THE DOOBIE BROTHERS — 00119670 / $16.99
VOL. 174 – SCORPIONS — 00122119 / $16.99
VOL. 176 – BLUES BREAKERS WITH JOHN MAYALL & ERIC CLAPTON — 00122132 / $19.99
VOL. 177 – ALBERT KING — 00123271 / $16.99
VOL. 178 – JASON MRAZ — 00124165 / $17.99

Complete song lists available online.

Prices, contents, and availability subject to change without notice.

HAL•LEONARD® CORPORATION

7777 W. BLUEMOUND RD. P.O. BOX 13819 MILWAUKEE, WI 53213

www.halleonard.com

1114